A Promise to
JESS

SEAN GRAHAM

A Promise to
JESS

The Journey

iUniverse®

A PROMISE TO JESS
THE JOURNEY

iUniverse books may be ordered through booksellers or by contacting:

iUniverse
1663 Liberty Drive
Bloomington, IN 47403
www.iuniverse.com
1-800-Authors (1-800-288-4677)

ISBN: 978-1-5320-1555-7 (sc)
ISBN: 978-1-5320-1556-4 (e)

Library of Congress Control Number: 2017902849

Print information available on the last page.

iUniverse rev. date: 03/06/2017

The Journey

*T*hese wonderful kids took us on a journey with their football team. Living and writing about this time spent with these children was very riveting, exciting, unpredictable, rewarding and so much more. This story is viewed from a father, coach, mentor, friend and sometimes a passenger. In all roles, it was extremely uplifting to me.

Introduction

Writing this story was very inspiring to me from every day living this journey was a breath of fresh air. From this hum drum day to day grind, evenings and weekends spent with these kids become an oasis of excitement and anxious anticipation from week to week for all involved.

The team and these kids were an escape from life and a golden opportunity to relive my youth through the eyes of these children. Uncomplicated, nonjudgmental or unbiased were these kids. Our perceptions and views become distorted as we reach adulthood. This journey and these kids allowed me as well as their parents to enjoy and revel in their excitement. Innocence and a carefree outlook taken by these kids was refreshing and self gratifying to me. I am sure the same for their parents as well.

Living the journey and then writing about this story was very rewarding to me personally. In such a competitive atmosphere, perspective was always attained when seeing this all through the children's eyes. Simple, innocent, unassuming and enjoying every step no matter how intense it got.

These children trotted on and lead us down their magical path. Most times completely oblivious to the surrounding distractions I feel they taught us all a valuable lesson. The "K.I.S.S." theory-Keep it Simple Silly. Thanks kids!!!!!

Preface

*I*was so moved and inspired while living this journey with these kids, I began to write about the story when the season ended. It was so easy to recount the moments whether they were high or low. Reliving the roller coaster ride as I write was as exciting as living through the story.

Acknowledgement

irst and foremost, I would like to thank these children all of them, as they hold a little place in my heart and memories. Thank you kids. As well as my son Jesse for his fortitude and willingness to stay the course. Keeping our motives and intentions a secret between us.

The parents for their support and positive encouragement to these children. The coaches mostly for putting up with me and my high energy enthusiasm. My wife Kimberley again for tolerating me. I was a handful at times by my own admission. The league, their officials and the many volunteers. The football club and all who supported our football team.

Again Jesse for his artwork and illustrations and his spirit of the game and his faith in me.

Contents

Chapter 1

Introduction

Buzzzzzzzzzzz went the alarm and up and at em as I hit the buzzer I shook myself awake. I looked in the mirror at myself and gave that stupid smile and screamed "Time for Some Football."

Up the stairs I flew to find the slumbering troops where they lay strewn all over the living room floor. I stopped and looked out the window and realized that our string of luck with the weather had been broken. It was somewhat overcast and cold. I turned on the weather station as I sipped my morning coffee and decided to let the boys rest a bit longer before I began the madness.

The weather report said it was minus 27°C with the wind woo hoo! I turned off the T.V. and looked again at the boys resting and I began to scream.

"Everybody up and atom, its time for football boys."

The boys began to stir and like zombies began to rise as I was yelling in their faces, their team's fight song.

Jacob got up and headed for the solitude of his mother she slept in another room because she knew how crazy Saturday mornings had become around this house.

I yelled at Jess "It's time son, lets get to the zone and get pumped and ready, for today is the day."

I could not stand the adrenaline or the rush, I was wired I had to get the kids ready and get outside in the open air.

I fed Jess and Kurt and then the boys got dressed in their equipment and they slowly began to look like the Warriors who had just fought their way threw all kinds of adversity to get to this day. The city championship game. Jess began to get quiet as we applied the war paint to his face, I knew this was Jess's time to find the zone before the big game.

Kurt, well Kurt was beginning to learn to get quiet and allow his crazy Dad to rant and rave as they both knew it was Dad's way of getting mentally prepared.

We got dressed and headed out the door to pick up Kyle our lead blocker on offense. Kyle was just as wild as we were and we all headed to the field together as we yelled at each other in the van and pumped it up. I took a moment to realize that this was the last time I was going to drive these poor kids crazy and the last time this year that I would have the privilege to coach them in a game.

We had worked hard to get to this point. It was a one game winner takes all affair and we were meeting our newfound rivals the Bengals.

I began to reflect a bit as the kids were driving each other crazy in the van. I thought how seven short weeks ago these kids were winless and being beat badly. These kids were becoming the doormats of this league in the first half of their season. 0-3 in their first three games of the season and winless in their pre season. Then their offensive coach gave me the reigns and asked me to take over the offense and try to develop a working unit out of this rag tag bunch of misfits.

Well I accepted the challenge as did these kids and now after winning 5 of their last 6 outings. Unbelievable I was thinking as I looked in the rear view mirror at these little tigers.

I would now like to introduce myself and explain the beginning of how I found myself being part of what I feel to be the most memorable summer of my life.

My name is Sean Graham and all my adult life I have loved the game of football. In my youth as I came from a poor family of 16 kids, the opportunity for sports was never there for myself or my siblings.

I think my parents had their full of it just keeping the family going from day to day. Therefore, I spent most of my youth hanging around my brothers and friends and learning of life on the streets. Trouble and excitement and what some would consider a misspent youth was the order of the day for me.

I met my future wife Kimberley, who I had met a few years earlier but had not thought of her much over the last few years. When seeing Kim, I remembered the feelings I had always had for her. Kim and I talked and I began to fall deeply in love with Kim.

We began to date each other and everything seemed so natural between us. Kim had made me feel like everything for me was complete and we had decided to live together.

So after about 4 years of living with my guardians and struggling through some major changes in my life we moved in together and set up shop in a cute little apartment. Things went along very well and I believed us both were very happy. Kim had come from a similar background as I had and seemed to want the same out of life as I did.

I had never imagined myself as a father let alone a husband but I was in love with Kim and wanted to spend my life with her. We had a lovely wedding ceremony and an unforgettable honeymoon together. I remember the day after we got married I left my newly wed wife to go watch a football game with her consent of course.

After the honeymoon life went back to normal with Kim and I, now as the Grahams. Then came the next step in my life we had talked and decided to have children. I firmly believed with Kim and I and her support and love having children would be a wonderful thing.

Kim became pregnant in 1984 and we were both excited, my feelings were that this child would be a blessing for us. I have to admit here that secretly I was hoping for a boy and I know Kim well she was pulling for a girl.

My ultimate fantasy was that I could give my son the opportunities to play football or other sports, the chances I never had in my youth. I wanted to be able to show my children with Kim's help what I felt was the proper way to have a family. I was willing to try to be the father I felt every child should have, a tall order to fill for sure.

The day came with no real complications, Kim and I were thankful for this. Kim was a real soldier through the birth she was one tough woman. The feelings I had of Kim as a mother were to prove true as Kim quickly became a very caring, nurturing and loving mother to our child Jesse.

A couple of years passed and Jess grew into a strong healthy toddler. Jess was so quiet and well behaved, I could not believe he was a child of mine.

Things were going along fine with all the adjustments and all Kim and I felt that everything had gone so well, why not try again. So we did and Kim became pregnant again. Now I know I had my boy but a second son would be incredible, Kim was hoping for the perfect family, a boy a girl.

It happened in 1988 out came Kurt the Burt and if it could be possible he was as beautiful as the first. We involved Jess as much as possible in the process, it was his brother and baby Jess would tell us. I felt bad for Kim and her wanting a little girl, two tries and two boys geez that bothered me.

We now had Jess and Kurt at home and all the while I had these two taking over the world of football with me in the future. A year had passed and again Kim was in delivery with our third child.

Out came Jake the snake, Jacob was the final piece in the brothers three and he was just as beautiful. I smiled at Kim and expressed my delight but apologized that we did not have a girl. Then I said very clearly "The buck stops here."

The years began to pass and I counted them as our family grew, the boys were something else to watch, as they developed their own little personalities and characters. As they entered school I patiently waited as they grew into young gentlemen, I waited for Jess to reach the age for football. The boys now were playing in other sports such as soccer and T-ball and this was an exciting time for me and the boys.

I could see some real physical talents come out of the boys while they were playing and was proud of each of them. All the time Kim keeping her watchful eye on me and enforcing the boys' right to choose the sport they desired. I agreed and all I asked for was the chance to expose them to my game.

Chapter 2

Jess's First Season

The day finally came, Jess was of age and the time had come to bring Jess out to sign up for the game. I explained to Jess that I would be with him all the way through the practices and games. I knew football would be a new experience for him and can be somewhat intimidating, not to mention that I have waited nine years for this day.

I had a lot of confidence in Jess as he had displayed to me a very strong will and character. He was a very confident young man and I felt he had the tools to play.

I found out about the team in our area, so we headed out to the small park and practice field which was to be home for Jess and his teammates for the next 2 years. We wandered into this tiny shack at the field resembling a childhood clubhouse. Inside were all the coaches to all the levels of football, the coaches sporting all the team colours and insignias it was an impressive sight to me and Jess.

I smiled at and said, "Let's do it son."

I introduced Jess and myself to the table of coaches we signed Jess up and I asked a few questions about where, when, etc. The coaches were very receptive and the atmosphere amongst the coaches was one of excitement for the upcoming season.

Jess was very quiet and shy and I think a bit nervous. One of the coaches tried to talk to him and it seemed to relieve Jess somewhat. We received all the information we needed and headed out as we drove home

I asked Jess what he thought. He told me he was impressed and was excited about playing.

About 2 weeks later we headed out to this warehouse to meet the coaches and get Jess his equipment. Jess was all excited about getting his own helmet and uniform and so was I. When we arrived at the warehouse he was outfitted.

While Jess was inside I watched the other kids run around with their new equipment half on, it looked so cool.

Jess came out sporting his new uniform and equipment, I smiled and told him he looked like a real ball player. Jess smiled at me and I could hardly see his little face inside the huge helmet, he recognized some of the other kids playing and ran over to play. I was happy he had some friends on the team this would help him the kids played for a while, I called Jess and we headed home. The coaches told us to show up at the little park with equipment on for our first practice.

We showed up the next evening at the tiny park for practice and Jess was all decked out and looking cool.

The little park these kids called home was a small patch of grass between a play structure on one side and a tennis court on the other side. It was quaint and not much but it had character. As well, what a name for a football team I thought to myself the Warriors, I loved it.

Jess went out on the field and joined the other players as they played around Waiting for practice to start I headed over to the sideline and sat down. The coaches introduced themselves to everyone and began the practice. As I watched the kids it made me think of that movie The Little Giants, they were quite the crew. I saw all the other parents of the kids would gather and socialize on the sides. Jess was blending in with all the kids but I could see he was a bit nervous about it all, I could not blame the little guy. I knew he could handle it he was a very strong inner person.

I watched the kids and talked to a few of the parents on the sides as I knew some of them but mostly kept to myself as I wanted to watch the kids. After practice Jess and I headed home I had a good talk with Jess about what he thought of the team, to my delight he was very excited about the team, game and the coaches.

We began to show up for practices every night and quickly got into the routine and the program and we were both becoming very much involved.

I think that over the 2 years I am writing about here Jess only missed one practice and never missed a game. I just wanted to mention the conviction he displayed to me. As Jess would practice, I would mingle a bit with the parents and watch the practice. The coaches seemed to have a good grasp of the game. They also seemed to communicate well with the kids, which I felt was important.

I would like to gloat a bit here now, I felt like I was in seventh heaven I could watch the game I love from the grassroots, the average age being eight or nine. As well you have to realize that for most of these kids it is their first experience with this game. I imagined how difficult it must be on the coaches to teach this sport to these kids, football is a very demanding and complicated sport to play let alone teach to kids. I admired the coaches for their patience and commitment to these kids.

It became obvious to me that the team and program was a bit of a social event for the parents off the field. They would become involved with the kids, the coaches, and themselves, it was almost like they would adopt the team as 1 big family this pleased me. I was soon to learn exactly how tight knit this group would become over the length of the season.

Practice continued on, they were 4 nights a week at this little park for about a month straight while the kids and the coaches prepared for the upcoming season. On Saturday morning of the Labour Day weekend the first game of the season began. The season at the tyke level consists of six season games. Each game began on Saturday mornings either at the Warriors home field which was a beautiful football field at the local high school, or on the road. Then the Warriors would have to travel to another team's home field anywhere in the local area.

The parents and kids of both teams would meet at the designated field every Saturday morning. Under the direction of the coaches and league referees the kids would play out the game of football, it was great. The parents would cheer on their children both sides and get right into the game it was a lot of fun to be part of.

The season opener had come and myself, Jess, the parents, the team and the coaches were all ready. It was an exciting time the anticipation of all those weeks of practice would be put to the test.

The season began on a glorious Saturday morning the sun was bright and it was a beautiful fall morning, the field was so peaceful as we all began to arrive. Jess and I started this ritual in which we would arrive at the field early and walk together around the field and just talk about the game coming up.

I cannot explain how special this time was to me we would walk and talk to each other and just try to prepare Jess mentally.

I have always been one of those annoying morning persons who would wake up early and have enough energy to light up a city and to my pleasure Jess was now showing these same great characteristics. I enjoyed watching the morning mist coming off the field and I would make Jess aware of the beauty of nature, together we would watch the day wake up and unfold before us.

As the other parents and kids would show up Jess and I would watch as the field would come to life with the hustle and bustle of people. Kim would come along with Jake and Kurt later, as Jess and I were usually out of the house before they would awake we were to excited to sleep in. After all the set up with the refs and kids and coaches and parents the game started. Finally we were into our first season of football, it was all terrific and great to be a part of the 1995 Warrior football season.

I now feel that I have to try and briefly explain the game, the league and the rules a bit to you. It will help later in the book to understand the basic structure. We will return to the opening game.

As mentioned earlier the Warriors are 1 of a number of Tyke teams in the city league. The season consists of 6 season games over a 6 week period, every Saturday morning with practice in the week between the games after a summer of training camp generally 3 months.

After 6 games the regular season ends the points of all the teams are totaled. The teams with the most points go to an A playoff pool (round robin type affair.)

The top middle of the pack teams goes to a B playoff pool (round robin) and the lower ranked teams go into a C pool playoff (round robin).

After the points are calculated and the teams are placed a 3 game round robin affair begins for each pool A, B, C. The best two teams from each round robin affair meet in the city final game to determine the city champions for that division.

This in short is how the tyke season and playoffs is operated. I would like to explain the basic structure of the game so please bear with me.

The game consists of 4 quarters, meaning 4-10 minute quarters. Each team consists of 10 players on each squad being the offensive and defensive squad. As well, what I found to be great was that at this level the coaches were able to go out on the field with the kids and be right in the action sort of speak giving guidance.

The basic idea of the game is to have our offensive squad score a touchdown against the other team's defensive squad and vice versa, and the opposite squads on the other team tries to stop our team from scoring.

While our kids are trying to advance the ball the other team's kids are trying to stop us. When we finish with the ball by scoring or not getting the ball moved on the other kids, the other team gets the ball and there opportunity to move the ball against our 10 defensive kids. Then our job is to stop the other team from moving the ball on us for a score or first downs this process goes back and forth for the 4 quarters. After the 4 quarters the team that scores more than the other team, is the winner of the game

There are referees at all games in order to keep control of what is happening during the game. It is a bit of a rough game as the kids try to move the ball against each other through blocking, running and brute strength. The kids are all well padded and protected with equipment. Therefore, now that I have explained I hope it gives you a better understanding of what these kids go through in a game and a season. In addition, I would like to mention here the restrictions on this level of football. To the best of my knowledge, age is no older than 11 and as young as 6, the weight is no greater than 90 pounds for Tyke level. This keeps the league and teams with some parity. The other thing at this level is once the kids move up in weight and age they must move up to the other level and teams. Therefore, a kid could be a Tyke for anywhere from 1 to 3 or 4 years, as long as they stay in the weight and age limitations.

This is important to know, as I mentioned earlier this is to some kids their first experience at football, so these kids are true rookies to the game. As at other higher levels, when the kids move up they are considered rookies at each level in their first year. Yet these kids have played the game at the lower levels so they are rookies to the level but not the game. I hope you understand this because it is important to know. A rookie is a first time player and a veteran player is a 2nd or 3rd year player.

Obviously to play with veterans would be better than to play with rookies for the simple fact of experience, this is a very intimidating game. Rookies tend to panic and loose focus easily. I explained this to you as well because it will help in understanding the book and the courage of these kids.

The 1995 season kicked off in great fashion, it was a home game for the Warriors and everyone was there. The field had become a beehive of activities as the little soldiers went to war with each other and all the parents cheered the kids on, it was quite a weekly event.

Jess fit in well now we would attend all the practices through the week preparing weekly for the weekend games. The 1995 season for the warriors went along well the kids played well and were triumphant more than not, they had a good team with a lot of veteran players. I was happy for Jess and the kids and I thought to myself, it's better for Jess to start with a good team than a bad team. I felt it would be more encouraging to the kids as first time players.

I recall in this year I was talking to some of the parents at a practice and I had mention I would love to help coach the game to the kids. The team was doing well and at present there were only 2 coaches for about a squad of 28 kids. I thought I could help as well be closer to Jess, Anyway we all gathered for one of the final games of the season. It was being held at the other end of the city that Saturday. After all the cheering and the victory at this game, I proceeded to collect Jess from his team to go home and I approached the coach of the Warriors. I congratulated them on the victory as I always did, this is when I introduced myself and explained that I use to play football and told him I would love to help out if I could.

The coach was very receptive to me and told me I was more than welcome to help. I thought oh my God, I now can coach the game be right on the sidelines with the kids, it was like a dream come true. I could not wait to tell Jess and Kim, I grabbed Jess and we headed home. I told Jess the good news and he was happy for me.

We hurried home to tell Kim and the boys. Little did I realize at the time what this decision I had made was going to encompass but I was happy and excited about next week our first practice with me as an assistant coach.

We showed up at practice the next week I tried hard to blend with the coaches and help where I thought I could. I tried to work on mental conditioning and preparation with the receivers on offense they were great kids.

The coaches welcomed me in and I really appreciated this the coaches were encouraging and this helped. I tried to talk to the kids about how important concentration and focus was to the game. I tried to get the kids to think, focus, and pump them up emotionally. I blended in with the kids and the coaches and I loved it Jess and I would stand together on the sidelines in the games and be right in the thick of it. It was great, I found this one kid and I decided to work with him. I think he was the team's number one receiver. Well, I worked with the kid and took great pleasure in watching him become a great receiver right before my eyes. It was unbelievable to watch the kid get better.

I found them so easy to coach and such a pleasure to be around. I worked with another kid that the coach was trying to make into a receiver. This kid was fast but did not have the focus he needed to be a receiver, so the coach asked me to work with him. It was so rewarding when I watched this one turn into a great receiver, it was the confidence he lacked and when he found it he was incredible to watch.

This was my first real taste of coaching and I loved it. At this time I could not spend much time coaching Jess, as he was a rookie and did not play much. Even still I knew Jess would get his chance next year. The season ended and the warriors were headed to the playoffs as a top seed in the B pool. They told me that at this level the game was for fun and not competitive. I later learned on my own that some involved in this league believed very much in winning, whether they want to admit it or not.

I do not want to dwell on this much here but I think I first saw the competitive nature come out in the final game before the playoffs. If our team had won their final game we would have made the A playoff round. As it happened we lost this game and fell to a top seed in the B round. It was at this game that I got to see how competitive it was.

The playoffs began and the Warriors walked through the round and won the B cup city championship. I was so pleased for both the Warriors and Jess, the team did well and the parents were very proud of the kids. All in all it was a great season for Jess and myself, Jess had his feet wet and loved it and so did I. We reveled in the celebrations and attended the Warrior banquet with Kim and the boys and it was a great time for all.

At the banquet the kids got the praise they deserved, the trophies and the parents and all involved congratulated the kids for the great season they gave us. It was a somber feeling to realize the season was over for another year. Jess and I headed to the shack to hand in the equipment until next year. It was here that the head coach asked me if I would take over next year as head coach, I could not believe it, I readily accepted and told the coach I would be there for the kids. I thought all right I get the whole team to coach and can do things with all the kids instead of just the receivers, I was a bit nervous about the idea but I wanted to do it big time.

I told Kim and the boys the great news and Jess was really excited anyway I was to find out later that the head coach, who offered me the position was to retract this offer for some reason or another. He then extended an invitation to return as an assistant coach and I agreed. It rather upset me but I felt that I had to work my way up and it would take some time. We looked to next year both Jess and I.

Jess and I as a bonus we had Kurt to come out next year with us. Kurt was playing soccer in our area and had shown great interest in football as some of his friends from school were playing on the team and his Dad and brother were there. We had talked to Kurt and he was ready to play but he was still young. I knew as a coach and helping out, I could probably get Kurt in early and at this time I was not aware of the consequences of bringing in kids so young. The coaches told me not to bring in kids this young, but I did not listen and was soon to learn that the coaches were right.

During the off season I took it upon myself to enlist the assistance of a close friend of mine and asked him to bring his son out and help coach the kids next year. Dave had been a friend and a co-worker for almost 15 years and was a good family man and great with kids. The big bonus with Dave was that he loved football. As well he had played high school football and came from a football family.

His son was somewhat of a budding athlete that he could expose to the game. Anyway Dave agreed to sign up his son and help coach for the next year. All we had to do was wait for the next season to come.

Middle Addition

I would like to take a moment here to briefly explain the season, the games and the practices all in a structured timeframe for better understanding of the flow of the journey.

The second season began approximately June of 1996 and we would practice 3 days a week that included Tuesday, Wednesday and Thursday evenings from 6:00 p.m. to dusk this was training camp. Approximately the 3rd weekend in August 1996, our pre season would start and we would play Saturday mornings at 9:30a.m.

The season would begin early September Labour day weekend. So the season would be practice Tuesday, Wednesday and Thursday evening and the games held on Saturday mornings weekly. End of season would be after the 6 games, I will explain the playoffs when we reach that point in the story.

Chapter 3

The Beginning of the Second Season

The winter passed, Jess and I were excited about the upcoming season. As well, Dave and I had talked over the months about how we would like to try to teach, coach and help the kids. I remember Dave would constantly say

"Basics Sean, at this age we have to be as basic as possible with our plays and practices".

Dave and I headed to the park to sign up our boys and meet again with the coaches. I did not know at this time that one of the coaches was very intimidated by Dave.

I have to admit Dave is a big boy, big and burly and I guess looks kind of rough. After all Dave was an offensive lineman in High School. One of the coaches was not sure about Dave being around kids I introduced Dave to the coaches at the shack. I told the head coach I had invited Dave out to help coach and hoped that they did not mind. I explained Dave's experience the Head Coach welcomed Dave's help.

We were also told, that this season we would run the offense of the team and the other coach would run the defense. The Head Coach would oversee the operations as he explained to us as he wanted to sit back, take it easy and let us run the team. Dave and I agreed and expressed our interest in being introduced to the kids.

Registration went off without a hitch and the coaches assembled the team. Dave and I were not involved in this process. We showed up at equipment night to hand out the equipment and met some of the kids.

My hopes were high as practice began in early august Dave and I thought we could get completely involved right away. As it turned out the Head Coach took charge of the team and began practices with his game plans, strategies and formations. Dave and I just stood by the sidelines and watched with the parents as the two coaches began to coach the kids in practice. The new set of parents and kids for the year began to fall in place for the upcoming season. Jess felt comfortable and Kurt was in awe of it all. As with Jess I assured Kurt that I would be there every step of the way, this seemed to comfort him.

Practice began to go well and Dave and I hovered around on the sidelines and helped when we could. Now I would like to give the benefit of the doubt to the coaches. It seemed that what the coach had asked us to do was not going to happen. The Head Coach seemed to want to run the offense solely and the other coach wanted to run the defense. Dave and I were kind of confused and unsure on what our roles were with the team.

We just talked with the kids about basic techniques and structure. Now I do not know if the coaches did not trust us as they really did not know us. In turn, Dave and I were rookies to this program as well. However, I would like to say here that football is football and kids are kids. Dave and I being experienced in both felt we had a lot to offer. Instead of pushing the issue, Dave and I just went along with the system of practice.

While we went through these practices Dave and I would talk with the coaches both on and off the field. It was more off the field conversations that bothered me the most. The two coaches were in consensus that this year's Warriors would not do well in the season because the team was made up of rookies and young kids. We felt that the coaches were comparing this year's team to last year's team and this was unfair. The year before they had a veteran squad that was older and bigger.

Both experience and age was lacking for this team I rather agreed in principle but never in spirit, I was still very naive to this league. I often wondered about Jess and Kurt when the coach told me that this team would be lucky to win one game this season.

I often thought how could I tell my boys that winning or losing meant nothing that this season was a time to build. I did not voice my feelings against defeat before the contest and followed the program.

I could not bring myself to believe that these kids were not going to compete in this season. I have always been a firm believer that anything is possible if you want it bad enough. A positive attitude before going into any sport is the only attitude to have. The coaches were in charge of the team and out of respect for these coaches I held my tongue. I would discuss these feelings and direction with Dave and both Dave and I were of the opinion that anything's possible and we should not sell these kids short.

Practice continued along and the sides were being formed now and working well. I felt that the coaches were beginning to involve me slowly in the coaching and decision making and I appreciated this. The season was now upon us, a week away. The coaches handed out schedules to the kids and parents, Everyone was getting prepared for the season opener.

We entered the season as assistant coaches and what felt to be just another spectator. I remember attendance was a problem with the kids. I did notice a core of about 10-12 kids who would be at practice religiously. I knew that down the road these ones would be the kids to carry this team through the season and further, with any luck.

Now, these kids resembled a rag-tag bunch of misfits they were scared, unsure and not very confident in themselves. I could feel it and I am sure these kids and parents could feel it to. Dave and I thought all we could do was help coach, reassure and try to instill some confidence. After all the practices and time spent in preparation. The season finally came. The coaches felt prepared and the night before the 1st game the Head Coach made a good speech to the kids, which was fairly inspirational.

Saturday morning arrived and I was ready for some football, I do believe I was more pumped up and excited than the boys. I began what I found to be a good pre-game ritual I would walk into Jess's room first and I would scream "Are you ready for some football." I would dance and scream at Jess until he woke up, then I would go into Kurt's room and repeat the screaming. Amongst all this my wife, Kim would wake up with the noise and try to kick me out of the house. I would feed the boys their breakfast all the time verbally motivating them and getting them psyched. After the boys got dressed we would head out the door, to the pleasure of Kim and Jacob.

I loved Jess's reaction when I would motivate him. He would stare at me in disbelief and Jess would just get quiet and angry and would begin to focus in. When Jess got quiet, I knew he was getting pumped. It took Kurt a little while to blend into our pre-game ritual. We would get to the field where we were playing about an hour or so before the game started. I would get Kurt and Jess to walk all around the field and get familiar with it.

The field was always so calm and serene when we arrived, we were always the first to show as the coaches would ask the kids to come at 9:00 for a 9:30 game start. I did not think this was right but the coaches were in charge. I felt the kids needed at least an hour to wake up and get prepared. Coach Dave began coming early with us as well.

Well the morning progressed and the kids began to trickle on to the field. The parents would begin to gather on the sidelines and the field would begin to wake up for the contest ahead. Jess, Kurt and I were so excited waiting for the first game to start. The kids would do the exercises in their squads with the coaches preparing for the game. Once the referees got to the field the game would soon begin. Dave and I would talk a bit with the coaches in final preparation. The kids were excited and there would be approximately 100 people there to watch the game.

The game began and as did the unbelievable season that no one could have predicted. The game went along pretty well, you could tell the kids on both teams were slow and unsure. Our defense played well but the offense was slow and ineffective. This was to be expected as their is so much more timing and structure on the offensive unit. The half-time break came and to our surprise the Warriors were leading thanks to a defensive touchdown. The coaches, Dave, and I consulted at half time and the kids were pretty wired about their beginning. Dave and I would try to motivate the kids at half time while the coaches would discuss the game.

Half time ended and we began the 2nd half with a lot of confidence. While the team and coaches adjusted there plays for the 2nd half, the other team adjusted as well. It was not a very promising 2nd half. The other team bowled us over scoring close to 30 points. Not only were their kids beating our kids on the scoreboard, but also I felt our kids were being beat up physically on the field.

I felt so bad for the kids, especially for Jess. I can say Jess was trying his best but to no evail. All the kids were trying hard but this team was just too big, strong and experienced. The game ended with our Warriors not scoring on offense and being beat badly. At the end of the game, the Head Coach had a speech for the parents and kids who would gather around after the kids shook hands and congratulated the opposition. I saw a bit of taunting and teasing from the other team, It hurt me and I am sure it hurt our kids. I know this level was not to be competitive but I have always felt that if you do not want to be competitive then don't keep score or league standings. If the score was dropped then we could all go out on the field and have fun. I have been in sports long enough to know once a score is kept, it becomes competitive!

The coach's speech was reassuring, he told the kids he was proud of the effort they displayed and that the kids never gave up. This was just the first game of the year and they should not worry about it. The kids had their cokes which the coaches supplied after every game. The kids were kind of happy but I could feel the dejection. I would like to mention the coaching staff of the other team was very intense and competitive with their kids. It was becoming apparent that these other teams took this game very seriously. This was from the comments, tactics, and overall actions of the coaches on the other team I did not say anything I just kept it to myself.

After the kids and parents broke up and headed home Dave and I would talk with the other coaches and analyze the game and where the team needed more work next week in practice. We would break up and I would gather the boys and head home and I asked them what they thought of the game. Kurt would not be sure and Jess would say it was all right. I knew this was hard on Jess after playing the year before on a good team. I reassured Jess and told him to be patient and try hard and never give up. After talking with Jess, I kept thinking of how his coaches did not expect much this year. When we got home we asked Kim what she thought of the game. Kim, who was not sure what to think assured us to be confident and not to worry.

The boys stripped their equipment and went about their business. Jess's little buddy Kyle would come over to the house to visit with Jess after the game.

Kyle was the Center for the Warriors and he was a big boy for his age and a very good kid. We would talk about the game and I would get a bit of feeling about how the kids felt. Kyle was happy about playing but was not pleased about what happened. Later, on my own I would reflect on the game the kids and the team, I would try to figure out. What we should work on the next week at practice. I would mark down what I thought we needed to do and present it to the coaches on Monday. Until then, I would enjoy the rest of the weekend.

The litter
lasso

Chapter 4

The Promise to Jess

T
he weekend passed and back to Monday night practice at the tiny field, Jess and Kurt would run off and play with the other kids. I would talk with the coaches and offer my recommendations on what I felt the team needed to practice. The coaches seemed very receptive to my ideas and welcomed the input. The coach would blow the whistle and the kids would gather into their squads for warm up. I now began to walk through the formation of kids as they stretched and did their exercises. I was trying to get to know the kids one by one as I strolled around I would wink at each them, smile and say hello. I would also help with their equipment and anything else they needed.

The parents were watching their kids warm up, the overall atmosphere at the tiny field was one of subdued and quiet expectations. Everyone realized that Saturday past was the first game of the season, so I do not think many put much into the loss. Practice went on this week and we the coaches drilled the kids in the areas that needed work. Dave and I just wondered around and helped where we could. The week went along well as the kids were getting ready for their second game. I would like to revisit again the make up of this team since 18 kids of the squad were rookies and very small and young. I was quickly learning how small and inexperienced these kids were.

I still could not resign myself to the belief that these kids would not do well this year, Jess was doing well with the team and Kurt well Kurt can get along anywhere. Some of the kids were calling Kurt, Richie Rich, as he resembled the cartoon character Richie Rich, and had now inherited the nickname at both school and football. Kim and I had found that Jess always had a quiet affect where he went, but Kurt always had a profound affect on people. We both prayed that this was a blessing and not a problem.

I would like to mention one of the kids here his name was Brendon and he was only 6 years old. Brendon was a sweet little guy but we all thought at this age he was not mentally ready for the game and the coaches took him on the team as a result of a request from the league. I felt Brendon was too young but Kurt was only 7 years old and I pressured the coaches into allowing Kurt to play. Now I think it is good for the kids, at this age to be at the practices and around the team for upcoming years but to play, I did not think these young kids were mentally ready. Both Brendon and Kurt might not of had the physical attributes and the experience but did they ever show some heart and passion for the game this alone would prove to be vital.

It was so cute to watch these two practice and along with about 5 or 6 other kids that were young and small. However, it was to become obvious that cute was not going to cut it in the games. It seemed to me that the bulk of the kids on this team were going to be bullied and manhandled by the opposing teams in our games by bigger and more powerful kids on the other squads. This bothered me to no end and I kept it to myself and felt all I could do is try to keep an eye on these kids in the upcoming games.

The coaches were forced more or less to take these kids on the team, by the league and parents, like me who did not understand the game and the importance of age and size. This was the major reason the coaches were not expecting too much from this team this season. The overall theme at practice this week was the same with the exception of Dave trying to get the kids back to basic blocking and tackling and trying to simplify the game for the kids and Dave was right.

The coach made his speech to the kids on Friday night before the second game of the season. The speech was uplifting and a good pep rally. The kids seemed to respond well to the motivational part of the game which I made a mental note of. The kids were dismissed and told to come back tomorrow ready. As the kids left the coaches, Dave and I discussed the kids and the strategies for Saturday's game. After awhile we broke up and headed home. On the way home I asked Jess and Kurt how they felt? Both were excited about the game and I was happy, I again told the boys to play hard no matter what happens tomorrow.

Saturday morning came and once again I was up early pumped and ready to go, God how I wished I was playing instead of coaching. After my coffee I began the ritual of screaming and dancing in the boys room to wake them up. I then served the boys breakfast and they suited up and we were out the door.

For this game, I had asked Kim to bring along the video recorder so she could tape the game and we could watch the game after. As usual we arrived at the field first and we had noticed as in our first game, the opposing team was arriving early as well. We would walk our end of the field and begin to focus in on the field and the game. I was becoming annoyed at the tardiness of our team I felt we had to start showing up earlier at these games. I watched as the other team was fully into a warm up before our team would even arrive at the field. I made a mental note of this and decided I was going to raise this issue with the coaches.

Our kids began to arrive and the field began to awaken, the referees were in place and our second game of the season had begun. The team we faced today was a huge squad and a good one. The game began much in the same fashion as did our first game except the other team was leading at half time our defense was playing well but our offense couldn't move the ball. At half time the game was close and Dave and I tried to motivate the kids and compliment them on their play in the first half as the other coaches conferred.

We entered the second half of the game positive and we felt confident, well it did not take to long for the other team to adjust to us. The second half was brutal for our kids they played hard but again our Warriors were overpowered and beat, on the scoreboard and on the field. The score was very unflattering to our kids and our offense still had not scored a touchdown now in two games. At the end of the game, the kids all met on the field to shake hands. I admired this team for its respect towards our kids, there was no taunting or teasing towards our kids and the game it self was clean and well played my hat was off to this team.

Nevertheless, the pain of defeat again was ever present I looked over at my little Jess and I could see the hurt in his eyes but he would not get angry, he would just continue and I admired this in my son. As for Kurt, well Kurt was happy to be amongst his friends he was not really in tune with what was going on. I was worried about Jess I felt the hurt for our kids, but there always has to be a loser. I kept telling myself this and until now the kids, the parents and the coaches were all taking this well but I could sense their concern.

The coaches handed out the cokes again and the post game speech was to be made. The parents now were gathering around to hear the speeches and to I think console their kids. The speech was good, the coach thanked the kids for their hard play and assured the kids not to worry as things would get better. After the speech, we chatted with the coaches about the game and then we headed home.

I smiled at Jess and Kurt and told them that this was not going to be the way all season I told the boys we had to have faith and continue with a positive attitude. All the time in the back of my head, I was beginning to question our team its heart, its commitment and its fight. I don't think Kurt was too upset but I think I was questioning the teams ability to compete and this bothered me. I felt so helpless with my son and his team, I did not know what to do. I thought all I could do was continue with the positive reassurance and plug along with the kids.

When we got home I smiled at Kim and told her it would get better. Kim was okay with the loss of the game but was concerned with how the kids felt. Kim was great she would remind us of the bright spots and would actually cheer us up. Jess and I grabbed our first videotape of the game and anxiously put the tape on to watch. As usual Jess's friend, Kyle had come over and we sat down to watch the game. We watched the game together a few times and talked about what had transpired on the field. We would laugh when we could and try to understand what was wrong with the team.

After the tape, Kim and the boys would go about their weekend and I would watch the tape and try to analyze what I could for practice next week. I began to become obsessive with analyzing every play and every kid but I felt this was needed. I had to understand for my own personal curiosity. I also wanted to get into the team, the kids and the game. Mentally I wanted to help and I wanted to figure out how.

I had decided to keep my thoughts to myself on the time our kids were showing up for the games. I decided I would discuss this at practice next week and I was determined that at least this would change. We may get beat repeatedly but come hell or high water we were going to be awake from now on. At this time I was feeling frustrated, helpless and not sure of what to do. I thought we would start small with an earlier start for the games.

I think at this time I was rethinking the philosophy of playing the game for fun and not to get to competitive, after all they are only kids. I also firmly believed that part of the fun of a game is being able to compete in a game and competing in my opinion was not what our kids were doing. I felt our Warriors were being humiliated on the field and I felt a lot of the reason was our lack of size, inexperience and youth.

Two games and two different teams, it was obvious to me now that our kids were out sized and out played. I felt we had to change something or the coaches might be right, we could go the season with only one win. I was now realizing that my sons were about to become the doormats of this league I still believed in our kids and believed in myself but something had to change I was not sure what. I felt that all I could do was take it one step at a time and help as much as I could. I finished watching the tape for I think the tenth time and I turned it off and went about my weekend.

Monday nights practice rolled around and I handed the videotape to the coach and told him I would give him the tape of the games from now on at practice Monday. I made my few recommendations and began to express my concern about the time the kids were showing up for the games. I explained that I would be there an hour before each game to warm up and run drills with the kids. I told the coach that I felt that the kids did not have enough time to get focused for the game. I explained to the coach that this was something I wanted to do and assured the coach that I would be there to greet the kids in the morning. I then finished by telling the coach that I would have the kids all prepared and ready for his arrival to take over.

The coach agreed and told me he did not mind if the parents and kids did not mind. He told me to go clear it with the parents who were socializing before practice on the side lines.

I walked over to the parents and with a nervous shake to my voice I asked for their attention. I was not sure how the parents would react, as the feeling at the little park this night was becoming increasingly anxious but I thought I have to start somewhere. I looked at the parents and I could see in their faces a sense of bewilderment. Most knew only the two main coaches who were running the team and I'm sure some wondered who I was and what was my role.

I expressed my concern about the start time and asked if from now on the kids could be at the fields earlier. The parents looked at me in an expression of approval the parents agreed. It was almost like they had expected something to change or happen. To my delight I had the coaches and the parents agreeing to this change. I felt this was a good sign and a start.

The coaches had begun practice and I had a small sense of accomplishment. We were now going into the mid-point of our season, our third game. Our little Warriors were 0 and 2 and I felt had not much to look forward to. As well, the kids were looking for their first offensive touchdown of the season. I had the belief if they could score just one touchdown it would benefit the kids greatly and possibly give them something to shoot for.

I always believed that winning was an attitude and had to be learnt and once a team learnt how to win, winning would be easier or at least obtainable. The other side of the coin is losing and losing is an attitude as well. Once a team learns to lose, they find a way to lose. I thought we have to teach these kids to be positive and believe they can win a game. I mean really believe. I think what I was feeling now was these kids had no heart or this team really had no character and it was time to find a character and teach them the passion for competition. I did not know how to go about creating this passion in the kids. I thought, I'm just going to start getting closer to the kids and start trying to pump them up and get them excited about playing this game.

The atmosphere at practice this week was still relatively subdued, but the tension I could feel was beginning to mount amongst everyone. On a whole the kids didn't really let it bother them but I could see there was that core of kids I had mentioned earlier in the book, my Jess being one of them were not taking this well. I noticed more frustration among the older kids and some animosity building between some of the kids this concerned me.

One of the older kids I speak of that was taking this badly was the feisty little Justin this kid had the heart of a lion and the competitive nature for all. He was a good kid but tough and had a lot of pride, which I think was being tested. I could see him venting out his frustrations at the younger kids. I intervened and we settled it right away. I began to explain to the kids that they were teammates, like brothers and or sisters and that they were to take care of each other. I admired this kid Justin because he had the passion and the spirit to lead this team if he chose to and at this time Justin was sharing the quarterback duties with this other fiery kid, Bosco.

Along with Bosco, there was Jess and a hand full of kids who wanted to change what was happening to their team. Practice continued as well as could have been expected it seemed that Dave and I were being more involved with the coaching and we both appreciated it. We worked on the offense most of the week as this was the area that we all felt needed work.

We stuck with the same playbook and tried to add a few changes to help the kids out this Saturday. On the final night of practice the coaches had their speeches again and tried to reassure the kids before tomorrow's game. The coach emphasized that this was considered a rebuilding year for the Warriors and it would be tough and that we should not expect too much. The speech was great and at the end the coach dismissed the kids.

The parents gathered up their kids and headed out, I watched as the parents and kids walked away and I felt so helpless. I could see that the parents were not sure what to expect anymore and were still hoping for their kids and the team. I thought to myself, no parent comes out and enjoys watching their children get beat repeatedly. I was a parent and I will be honest, I was not enjoying it at all. I did not agree with giving up on the season but it was going to be a tough haul for these kids and I knew Dave was becoming frustrated as well but I knew we could not give up. Dave, the coaches and I discussed the game plan again.

The little park was dark now and quiet after the discussion we all headed home and awaited tomorrow mornings game. We were playing one of the first place teams in the league tomorrow and we were all trying to be positive. The coach had told me we would not have a very good chance against this team tomorrow, as they were big and good. I did not like hearing this from the coaches, granted these coaches knew these teams better than I did but I didn't care how good any team was. I always believed any team can win on any given day, it's a game of emotion.

I thought instead of worrying about the other teams, lets worry about our team we have to try and have confidence in our kids. I headed home with my boys, I smiled at Jess and Kurt and then asked Kurt how Kyle was.

If you remember, Kyle was Jess's buddy that came over after the games. Kyle also happens to be the biggest kid on our squad.

Well when I looked at Kurt I remembered the hit Kurt put on Kyle in practice. Kurt being one of the smallest kids, it was like David and Goliath. I was watching the kids scrimmage and as the play came down field I watched as the play ended I saw Kyle storming back to the line of scrimmage and he was visibly upset, all I could think of was who was the unlucky kid that hurt Kyle.

I followed Kyle to play peacemaker and out of the crowd stood little Kurt and he knew Kyle was coming for him. I had to laugh, Kurt looked straight at Kyle and said as Kyle was pointing his finger at him.

"I'll do it again, Kyle."

Kurt was so determined and stood his ground, although he was dwarfed standing in front of Kyle. I broke it up and I had to smile as Kurt just shrugged it off and returned to practice. I asked Kyle what had happened and he told me that Kurt had hit him in the stomach with his helmet on the block. I tried to explain to Kyle, that Kurt was so small that was about the only place that he could have blocked him. Kyle calmed down and took it in stride.

Anyway, after all that happened Kurt said again to me in the van that he would do it again if he had to, I laughed and took the boys home.

Saturday morning came along and so did the screaming ritual in the Graham household I tried to fill the house full of energy for the boys to wake up to and absorb. Once again to Kim's delight we headed to the field but this day was going to be different I could feel it. We had the kids coming early and the kids would be awake and ready to play, today there was something in the air an aroma of change I could smell it. We got to the field and this being our second home game we arrived earlier than normal, awake and ready.

I had already extremely pumped up Kurt and Jess and I was waiting for any other little Warrior to come along so I could pump the hell out of them as well. We waited anxiously to see if the kids and their parents were going to respond to my request for an early start.

Dave and his son Gregory showed up around 8: 20 and I was pleased and we all began to walk the field together. I remember thinking this is the way it should be, all of us focusing together. To both Dave's and my surprise the kids began showing up early and I felt relieved. It was here that I realized that the parents wanted a change as badly as we did. I looked at Dave and I said,

"Now that we got them, let's get to work."

Dave and I began to get the kids into their squads right away. The other team began to arrive and I was so pleased to see that the Warriors were the first on the field this time, especially it being our home field. We were pumping up the kids as they stretched and I made a point to go up to every Warrior coming on the field and I would yell.

"Good morning."

If the response was lame, I would walk right up to the kid and scream. "GOOD MORNING HOW ARE YOU TODAY?"

I woke up a few of the kids. When I saw the kid was awake, I would smile and say.

"Now are you ready for some football?"

The little beggars would then reply in a shocked expression.

"Yes."

Then I would bellow out.

"I can't hear you."

The Warriors would scream yes back to me or I would continue this until the kid would. I wanted these kids awake today and ready. After I harassed the poor kids, I would send them over to Coach Dave to join in on the squads. I do believe some of the parents on the sidelines were not too sure what to think of Dave and my approach. Both Dave and I felt it was time for some discipline and order and it was also time to find out exactly which of these kids had the heart for the fight and which didn't. The kids seemed to enjoy the new regime and so did Dave and I. As the kids warmed up, Dave and I pumped up the kids with a constant barrage of positive reinforcement.

When the coaches arrived the kids were awake and ready to go, Dave and I turned the kids over to the coaches and blended back in. I think we surprised all with our methods as well the two coaches. I recall hearing one of the coach's say to the other, "It's like a damn boot camp". I smiled when I overheard this and I thought, your right its time for change, structure, discipline and some motivation and I was going to be damned if I was the only one walking around here wired in the mornings.

I had enough energy to share with all and I was going to share it with everyone whether they liked it or not. I loved looking into the little eyes of these tykes inside their helmets when I would yell.

"Good morning, open up your little eyes so I can see them in there."

The coaches spent the last few moments with the kids as Dave and I looked on, the coach made the game speech and the refs were in place. The game about to begin, God, I loved it. At this moment the coach came up to me and looked in my eyes and said are you ready to go out on the field with the kids today and take charge. As I had mentioned the coaches go right out on the field with the kids and coach as they play.

This coach had caught me completely off guard, I think this is why I was so involved in practice this week. I wasn't prepared to coach the kids with his offense, I told him I can't take over I don't know your system well enough or your plays to go out and lead these kids on the field. I can't recall what he replied but he turned and took to the field with the kids. I know he understood but I felt so bad, here I was looking for a chance to help and when it was offered I refused. It was a horrible feeling I could see he was reaching out for help and I was so helpless.

The kids did well in the first half, holding their own against this top team. At half time the other team was leading, but we were close. Again the defense of the Warriors was strong but the offense still could not score. After the half time break and a shot of motivation to the kids, the teams were back on the field and as before our kids could not hold on.

In the second half I could see that our coach on the field was exasperated, the offense could not do a thing. At one point in the second half our quarterback threw an interception as the other team's kids were running the ball back to score against us. I could see that our coach on the field had missed all the action as the kids ran by him. The coach was bent over with hands on his knees looking to the ground and shaking his head in disgust. It was tough to watch at this point, I knew the coach was done and so was the team.

He resembled to me a fallen hero wounded and defeated and it pulled at me. I cannot blame the man, it was a tough season and it was not getting any better. I thought to myself it must of been killing him inside, I was angry with myself for not being able to help the kids or the coach. At this time in this game, the whole team had come undone, that old saying of the wheels falling off the cart really applied here.

The opposition team was really taking it to our kids now both physically and emotionally it was like a small fire at first as the other team took over the game and the fire blew into an inferno. The score was getting higher for the other team and the hits were getting harder as the other kids could sense the confusion on our side just like a pack of wolves when they smell the blood and the fear. Dave and I were pleading with the kids from the sidelines to block and to play harder but it was no use. Even the parents of our kids were pleading from their side of the field to play with some heart. I think at this point there was nothing any one could do, it was apparent our kids were going to take a beating for the rest of this game and be humiliated one more time.

The point in this game when I got really upset, was when right in front of our bench the feisty Justin I had mentioned earlier got hit carrying the ball and hit hard. I felt there was no need for the intensity from the other team as they had the game well in hand. Justin fell down in front of us and began to cry and curl up in the fetal position. The coaches and refs ran to Justin, it was a while before Justin could be helped off the field. During all this Justin was crying in front of all of us.

Justin gets
hurt
They show'd no mercy

Well this seemed to horrify our little ones. I got angry and looked at one of our bigger kids standing beside me and said. "Look, look good, that's your friend on the ground crying there. You kids have to start blocking and playing this game with some heart. You kids can't keep letting these teams beat you up like this. You got to start fighting back."

I then told him.

"Get out there on the field and start blocking and show me some passion."

I think I scared the hell out him and he just looked at me and scoured behind the smaller kids who were huddled on the sidelines together, watching Justin. I looked at Justin and watched as he was carried off the field and I thought to myself, most of the pain was his pride.

As the game continued, the other team continued to physically have their way with our kids. I remember worrying about Jess out on the field and prayed he would not give up or get hurt. I could not blame the kids on the other side as the point of the game was to win and it was a physical game. I kept an eye on Jess and decided to keep to myself on the sideline, as I was becoming very agitated.

I recall hearing one of the parents from the sideline call out to our Warriors "Come on kids play with some emotion." It seemed like all the other noise and confusion around us stopped as this one plea for the kids carried across the field for all to hear. It only lasted a second, but it seemed an eternity and I could hear and feel the pain from this father. This plea stuck in my head for the longest time.

I looked over at the parents and could see the pain on their faces as they watched their kids get batted around one more time and as for the Warriors, it was sad. I could see now that some of the kids did not even want to come off the bench to go into the game at all and you could not blame them.

The game was winding down but the other kids were still hitting as they were enjoying their victory and I hoped that there would be no taunting after the game. I looked into the eyes of one of our smaller kids standing by me, and the fear, the youth, the inexperience and lack of size was in full view for the whole world to see. It was horrible, the game finally ended. I was not sure how much more the kids, the parents as well as myself could take of this, I felt relieved as the game had finally ended.

I watched the kids shake hands with the other team, I watched as some of the other kids were teasing our kids and this was tough to swallow for me. I could not fathom how our kids felt being the ones getting teased after the beating on the field.

Our little Warriors were now at the half way point of their season and their record was 0-3 and they seemed headed nowhere. The team still had not scored a touchdown and their future looked pretty bleak. I saw Jess come off the field and I smiled at him to try to comfort him a bit but I think Jess now had his fill too. He did not say anything he just got quiet and stood there and waited for me, as did Kurt. The kids and the parents gathered around as the other team celebrated on their side of the field you could hear them cheering and the excitement from their parents and coaches.

I do not remember the coach's speech after this game, as I was not really listening to him. The speech was made and the cokes were handed out to the kids.

I watched and was a bit amazed that a good number of the younger kids seemed unaffected by the game and the drama. Yet, it was here that I made a mental list of the kids that I could see were not happy. I felt these were the true players and I sympathized with these kids.

I said earlier that winning a game was not everything but competing was important to me. What I was witnessing from our kids was neither competing, losing nor winning, it was nothing. I cannot really explain what it was but I know I did not like it at all.

After the parents with the kids began to break up the coaches called Dave and I over to their van to talk. Dave and I just wanted to get out of there and leave it until next week at practice. We walked over to the van and began to talk. I could see that the one coach was visibly upset and I do not blame him. The other coach seemed to take it all in stride which was good. The coach looked at me and told me he was finished with the offense, he told me to write up a new playbook and choose which kids I needed to create an offense.

At first I was not sure what to say. The coach began to express to us how he felt burnt out after coaching for so many years and he felt the kids were not responding to him. He then added that maybe Dave and I could breath some new life into these kids. He explained the other coach was going to stay with the defense and asked me if I would take over.

I looked at the coach and asked him if he was sure he wanted us to take over and he replied.

"Yes, the offense is all yours now so bring a new play book to practice Monday."

I agreed to do it as I was thinking of jess and the kids, they needed something and I was not about to abandon them. I thought to myself that this coach must have some class and respect for the kids as I thought it must be difficult to turn over these kids to someone else. As Dave and the coaches talked, I thought that I would take over on the field with the kids next week and show them how to pump it up and play with some heart. Well I thought this is our chance to help these kids get some respect in this league. It was now time for these kids to start fighting back, stand tall and be counted.

The coaches packed up their stuff as we talked and took off for their weekend so Dave and I stood and talked as our kids played around. Jess, I had noticed went straight to our van and waited I knew we had to talk, I asked Dave.

"When should we meet to set up the play book?"

Dave replied. "I'm busy all weekend."

He did stress to keep it simple and stop handing the ball off, let the quarterback be our ball carrier from now on. I was a bit angry at first with Dave, but I realized he had other commitments that weekend. So I thought, what the hell I will write it up myself. We gathered up the kids and headed out from our field. I didn't talk much to Jess or Kurt as we all just sat there, I then turned to Jess and told him the news that I was now the offensive coach.

Jess smiled at me and said.

"I'm glad that you're taking over Dad."

This rather reassured me and I told Jess that I was going to change things around and things would be different. Jess gave me a look of relief and approval and it made me feel confident inside. We got home we talked a bit with Kim about the game and we then put on the tape of the game. We told Kyle the news that I was to coach from now on and Kyle seemed to approve of it as well and agreed we needed to change something. After a while, Kyle went home and Jess I were sitting there alone watching the tape as Kim and the boys were off somewhere. I turned to Jess and asked him how he felt about his team and the season they were having. Jess told me he was not happy with the losing but he still enjoyed playing the game and he really wished the Warriors could win a game.

This is when I looked at Jess and told him.

"Look into my eyes Jess."

I asked Jess. "Do you trust your Dad?"

Jess replied. "Yes."

I said. "All I ask is one simple thing from you and your teammates and that is that you start to believe in yourselves as football players. Believe in me and believe in the game plan we set up for you kids next week. Can you kids do this?"

He replied. "Yes."

This is when I made the promise to Jess.

I said. "If you kids can believe and have faith I promise the losing will stop son."

Jess smiled at me and we hugged each other. I told Jess that we were to keep this to ourselves this promise and work together to make it a reality. I told him.

"Do not worry no more, the losing stops here and now."

I told Jess to go about his weekend and we will leave it all until Monday's practice.

I felt so good after we talked I wanted so badly to give these kids something to hold on to or reach for, I did not feel helpless anymore about the situation. I felt if the head coach held to his word and allowed Dave and I to run the offense we were somehow going to get these kids to play football. I believed we were going to win and win big and I had to believe this for I could not sell it to the kids if I did not buy into it.

I spent a good part of the weekend setting up an offense that I thought was simple and could help these kids. I did not realize at the time the work, commitment and how demanding this job would be. I felt strong enough to help my sons and their team and establish some respect for these kids. My first thought was the only way to get some respect was to take it, these kids would have to play hard and win a game and commit as fully as Jess and I were willing to do.

I thought that the first thing I had to do was to reach these kids and show them how to win and at the least, show them how to fight in order to compete. It was to begin with Dave and I teaching these kids how to have some heart and belief in themselves, as well as passion to play and the desire to win. Self-respect and respect for the Warrior name needed to be taught. We eventually got the kids to nickname this the Zone, playing in the zone was to be mandatory from now on!

I will explain this later, I began to make a list of the kids I thought we needed and Jess headed up the list. I wanted Jess on the offense with me as we begin this journey together. I knew he had what it took to fight back and this was not going to be an easy battle.

I chose those kids that I had mentioned earlier in the book because as well as Jess, this handful of kids were the biggest and the ones that had displayed to me the heart for the battle to come. I was not excluding any one but we had one week to change and try to salvage a season. The more I thought about it the more confident I got with the idea. I anxiously awaited Monday night's practice to get with the kids and begin our journey together.

Chapter 5

The Change

*M*onday had come and I still was not completely prepared with the offensive structure. I had changed one thing the quarterback now was the principal ball carrier, no more handing the ball off keep it simple and cut down the mistakes. Remembering how young these kids were after creating 4 basic running plays for the quarterback I chose two other kids to help carry the ball when needed, essentially backups to give the quarterback a break or if he got injured. The first kid I chose was the biggest kid on the squad Kyle, I thought if we were going to run the ball, we were going to run with some power. The other kid was one of the smallest kid on the team. Avi, oh Avi could really run well but the best part about him was that he was so small I thought the other team would be lucky if they could see this little guy before he was gone.

I then took the next biggest kids, and lined them up in the backfield beside the quarterback. These two kids were to lead the quarterback through the line on the runs. These two kids would clear the way on the snap. For now these four basic plays would be all these kids would do and do and do, until the kids perfected this offense as well as wear down the opposing defenses. I thought if we kept pounding one spot of the other team's defense it would eventually give in.

So the strategy for our offense was to pound relentlessly one spot on the defense until the game ended or the defense softened enough for us to run through it. I truly believed this strategy would work if we could all be patient with it and allow it the time it takes to work. I knew it was simple enough for the kids and that they would be comfortable with it. I felt the only real drawback to this style of offense was that some people might find it a bit boring. Yet, I knew it would be effective and I felt that at this time it was not flair that we wanted, but results.

Along with the pounding we were to send as many lead blockers for the quarterback as we possible could, the idea was to out number the players at the point of attack.

The other element of our offense was to be the kicking game, which at present was not really effective at all. From now on we were going to kick the ball when we should and we were going to start establishing field position through the kicking game. We would get better field position for our offense to operate with, as well as take away field position from the opposing teams to help out our defense. I did not want teams to score quickly anymore against us because of our poor field position. Instead of going for our first downs on third downs, we were going to kick the ball from now on and make the other teams work for there points no more easy position for the other teams. I found from watching the league that not many teams used the kicking game effectively and I always believed that about 40 percent of your offense was the kicking game if it was used properly.

Basically all I did was simplify our offense as much as possible and try to develop the kicking game, in doing this I believed that these kids could almost eliminate mistakes which in turn would help these kids to compete. I decided that from now on, if you wanted to beat these kids, the other teams were going to have to beat them because we were no longer going to beat ourselves. That kind of football was over for these kids it was time to be focused and play error-free football.

The most important aspect of all of this philosophy was the motivation and the kids. I had to gain the trust of all these tykes and show them how to be confident in themselves and the game plan and have faith in themselves and me. I was not sure how to go about this and I knew it would be a task. I thought, all I can do is be natural about it and look at the team and the game through the eyes of these kids. I was going to have to get right down into the game with them and be a part of them both mentally and physically and stir things up.

I talked with Dave and asked him if he could take the kids back to the basics and teach the kid's basic blocking again. I had every confidence in Dave and his coaching abilities.

I then told Dave that I would work on the motivation with the kids as he taught the blocking schemes to our plays. I chose the kids I thought I needed to run this offense. It was not hard to find them because you could see the fire or the heart in their eyes. All of them had it but there was a handful of them that really displayed this to me. I thought I would start with them and hope it filters down to the rest and lead by example.

I showed up at practice Monday night with Jess and Kurt and as the boys took off to play I approached the coaches and presented my plan and strategy and my list of kids I needed. There was some concern over the kids I selected as about half of the kids I chose were presently playing defense. This meant to me that these kids were going to have to play both ways most of the game, kind of iron man football. I explained what I saw in these kids and stressed that I needed these kids. I thought these kids could play both ways if we asked them to. The coaches talked a bit and then decided to trust me and give my offense a chance.

The head coach then told Dave and I that we had tonight and Tuesday night to set this up. On Wednesday night, we were to run this new offense against the coaches and the defense of the team to see if it could be effective. I guess a trial run so to speak.

The feeling of the parents and the kids this night was one of confusion and dismay after the third straight whipping on Saturday past. I guess the parents and kids were rather expecting some kind of change, I sensed it in the air.

So far, the parents of these kids had been excellent, there were no comments or requests to change or any show of animosity towards the coaches and this made me kind of proud of these parents. Most of them, it seemed they were there for the kids and the team no matter what. The other coaches might have heard some grumbling from the parents but I do believe it was not significant. I thought to myself the commitment of the parents was essential to motivating these kids and turning this thing around and as it seemed the parents were there to support us and the kids.

As I was thinking this to myself the Head coach called all the kids in from playing to get ready for the warm ups. The coach asked the parents to come over and listen in as well. Once again catching me completely off guard. As soon as the kids and parents were gathered, the coach began to explain to all that coach Dave and I were taking over the offense of the team. From now on, the coach explained he was going to stand back and just coach the overall team operations and allow Dave and I a chance to operate the offense. The coach then told the kids to give us the same attention and respect as they gave him as coach. He then looked at me and said

"It's all yours, call out your kids."

I loved how he would put me on the spot but it was time now to take control. I admired how the coach addressed the kids and the parents on this issue. I think that he sensed that most of us were expecting some kind of change and the coach handled the situation very well in my opinion.

At this point the kids looked at me and were confused they did not know what to expect. I looked at Dave and smiled and began to call the kid's names off my list and told the kids to go down to the other end of the field and wait for me. It was kind of like a cloud of secrecy fell over the tiny practice field, as I finished calling out the names Dave and I headed down to the kids waiting. I thought the first thing was to gather the kids and explain. Therefore I called all the kids into a circle around Dave and I.

I began to explain to the kids the strategies and what was expected of them I was sure to talk slowly and confidently. I explained it in detail to them and assured the kids that we would take them through all of it step by step. I told the kids not to worry that Dave and I were there for them and if they had any questions, they were to ask us and not be afraid of us or the other players. I then began to tell the kids that this all depended on all of us working together as a team, trusting each other and believing in each other. I told them that it was like all of us being a family and we were all brothers and sisters. I then emphasized to the kids that they had to trust Dave and I and try as hard as they could to do what we asked and have some patience with the new offense.

After this speech, I was getting excited now I looked at the kids and said. "Are you ready to give this a try."

The kids replied. "Yes."

They seemed a bit unsure but this was to be expected. Other than a few, most of these kids did not really know Dave or I other than standing around and helping out here and there.

As Dave began to call the kids out for their positions, I stopped and called all the kids attention to me and said.

"By the way kids, this new offense is called "SMASH-FACE" and from now on we will smash face with whoever gets in front of us, do you understand?"

The kids looked at me in bewilderment as I was raising my voice and getting pumped up, the kids kind of nodded to me then I yelled.

"I can't hear you."

The kids then replied.

"Yes coach."

I smiled and said. "Then let's do it."

Once the kids were put into place we ran our first play Quarterback left and it went off okay as Dave and I walked the kids through the play step by step in slow motion.

I chose the feisty Justin to be the quarterback to run this offense as I believed in the kid that he was smart and tough enough to do the job, but only time would tell. I trusted my instinct about the kid I felt he was a leader and had the desire to lead and I felt this little tornado had it above the rest. I did this against Dave's wishes as he thought that Justin would have a tough time of it. We were going to demand a lot from this quarterback and I understood Dave's concerns but I just had this gut feeling about this kid and decided we would try Justin and if he didn't work out we would change.

We ran this same play repeatedly for about 30 times. I think the kids were confused about what we were trying to do. They were used to running an offense of about 10 different plays and admittedly, it was tough for the kids to do. This is why we simplified it for them. We then ran the other 3 basic plays with the kids and continued the repetition of the 4 plays. After we finished we told the kids that this was the offense from now on. We assured the kids that the plays would become like second nature to them and they would be able to run this offense in their sleep if they wanted.

I told them after they had perfected these plays we would introduce some more, but Dave and I made it very clear to the kids that no other plays would come until they were all completely comfortable with this. Dave and I told the kids to trust the plan and themselves, with the repetition of the plays they would perfect it.

Tuesday night's practice came and after the warm ups the same thing happened, we allowed the kids to practice their offense. I would like to mention here that the Coaches were being very good about turning their kids over to us and allowing the change to take place. The coaches took the other kids and Dave and I wandered away with our squad to the other end of the field. It seemed that the kids were beginning to buy into the plan. The kids ran the plays well and were looking comfortable with the formation. Dave and I continued to work on their battered egos, we kept things up beat and positive and constantly assuring the kids in themselves.

As we were in the huddle calling the play, I can't remember which kid began it but we all began to chant Smash Face, Smash Face, in the huddle. I thought this was a good sign. The kids were beginning to get motivated, in our next huddle I looked at the kids and asked them.

"Who Are We?"

The kids were not sure of what to say. I repeated myself and the kids just looked at me until finally one of the kids replied.

"The Warriors coach." I smiled and said.

"Right son and what do we do?" The kids again went quiet and one of them replied.

"Smash face." I smiled and said.

"Now you have it." I then yelled at the kids.

"Who are we?" The kids yelled back

"The Warriors." then I yelled.

"What do we do?". They yelled back.

"Smash face." I then looked at Justin and said.

"Then let's do it."

I am not sure what I had just seen in the kids by creating this chant but in retrospect I believe it was the heart of these kids coming to the surface. I knew it had to be nurtured and encouraged, they had the heart they just didn't know it.

I was pondering this a while as the kids ran the play to the pleasure of both Dave and I in the huddle again we did the chant and it seemed to create positive energy. I would look at Justin and say. "Then let's do it" and Justin would call the play to his teammates and the kids would run the play. I was becoming proud of this rag tag bunch but the big test was tomorrow when we had to run this offense against the other squad and coaches. I had confidence in this bunch but the reality is practice is one thing and scrimmage is another. All we could do was wait and try our best.

We ended practice this night and the kids were getting a bit confident in themselves. I approached Dave and asked what he thought and Dave's reply was.

"Don't worry about it, keep it simple and the kids will do okay."

Dave's ever-present confidence was great for both the kids and me. We talked with the coaches after the kids were dismissed and we all agreed tomorrow night we would unveil the new offense to the rest of the team and the parents. We finished our chat and Dave and I gathered up the kids and headed home.

Wednesday night came along and the anticipation was now at a head as the kids ran around and played.

I approached the coaches and asked them if they were ready to stop the new offense. The coaches chuckled and said.

"Let's give it a whirl."

They told me to set up and let them know when I was ready I was somewhat nervous about it. In the van on the way to practice, Jess had encouraged me by telling me not to worry and just run the offense we had created. I thought I had better be confident if I wanted the kids to be confident.

Warm ups had ended and the coaches asked if we were ready, I said.

"Yes."

Dave and I set up the kids as the other coaches set up the defense to stop us. All the parents had gathered around now to watch and it seemed that all eyes were on us. I got into the huddle with the kids, looked at the kids and smiled and said.

"It's now time to show these people what we can do, be strong and do what we showed you to do and have confidence in yourselves. I know you can do it and so do you let's Smash face, Justin call the play now."

Justin got into it right away and barked out the play to the kids in the huddle. I stood back and watched as the kids ran the play. It was a good run, not a great run but it was a positive run. I remember thinking to myself as the kids ran the play here we go this is the first of many to come. The coaches and parents watched and there was no real reaction after all it was the first run. I thought these people will see it once the kids run it a few times. The kids and I went back to the huddle and I looked at the kids and said.

"That was good kids, this time same play but give me some heart with it this time, get angry, get pumped."

I told the kids. "Don't just block these kids, smash them out of the way."

I raised my voice and said. "Justin call the play and this time kids let's show them some smash face football."

Justin barked out the play, the kids lined up and I stood back and watched. After awhile, our kids were beginning to move the other kids out of the way. It was becoming obvious to all that we were going to move the ball no matter how the coaches set up their defense against us.

The coaches began stacking their kids right in front of where we were running and our kids kept running the same play and were picking up more steam every play. I began to explain to the kids in the huddles about the rhythm of our offense. "Huddle up, pump it up, call the play and then run it, huddle up, pump it up, call the play and then run it and so on."

I was telling the kids in the huddle.

"If you can get a team moving backwards on your plays and you turn it into a rhythm it becomes almost impossible to stop. Once you get the team moving backwards don't stop until the team is in the next province or the whistle blows to end the game."

I believed that the rhythm I was telling the kids about was an important aspect of the discipline to play the game along with the theme of repetition. If the kids got the rhythm in a game and the offense moving it would be easier to keep the focus and more importantly ball control. I believed to be the most important strength of any offense. If we controlled the ball we then would control the game and this was to be the overall objective of this offense.

I was impressed with the kids, they were now running the ball at will and breaking through the spot we had chose to smash through even though the other coaches kept stacking kids in the spot. The kids were still breaking through. Along with myself I could see that the parents watching were impressed with the kids. Even the other coaches were impressed, although it was their defense we were now shredding up. I think most importantly that the kids were impressed with themselves, especially after three weeks of not being able to move the ball. These same kids were now running a successful offense and moving the ball at will, this was great for their confidence.

As we were running the plays, I recall one of the parents behind me commenting to another parent.

"I wonder if they have a play to go right."

I understood as all the kids were doing was pounding the left side of the defense I looked at Justin in the huddle and said.

"Okay kids, I want it changed a bit, it's the same play to all of you so do the same block."

I then told Justin. "This time Justin you run the ball the other way, run it right."

I asked the kids. "Do you understand?"

They all nodded. I asked. "I can't hear you."

The kids then yelled. "Yes coach"

I replied. "Let's pump it up kids."

I told Justin. "When you run son run like the devil because no one will be there."

Justin just smiled and called the play. I stood back and watched the play and it was beautiful, everyone went left and Justin went right and he was all alone. As Justin ran into the end zone after about a 30-yard run he ran by the coaches and laughed. The coaches chuckled and I turned to the parent who had made the comment and smiled and said.

"Of course the kids can run right, the kids like to set it up first." He just laughed.

After the score the coach called the practice, I think he was satisfied with what he saw. I could see that night these kids were going to kick some butt now and this I had no doubt of. The kids were happy and so were Dave and I as we had passed our first test. The kids did their warm down exercises and Dave I and the coaches gathered and talked.

The coaches showed some concern about the same play over and over again and both Dave and I stressed that this offense will work. You just had to be patient with it and stick with it, I told the coach," We can't abandon the strategy in a game even if it looks slow and ineffective. Eventually our kids will wear down the kids on the other team but we have to believe in the kids and the strategy. You have to trust us on this."

The coaches agreed in principle but I could sense the impatience of the coaches that night and I knew these coaches did not really understand. I felt that if we were given the chance, the kids and I would prove what we were saying. The practice broke up we all headed home and in the van on the way home I smiled at Jess and asked him what he thought of it all, Jess smiled and said.

"Dad just do it, you can do it and we can do it don't listen to anyone. Dad just do what you think is right and we will listen to you."

I felt so reassured as we drove home, I kept thinking the kids are right Sean, just do it.

Practice continued that week, we ran the same play repeatedly and we slowly showed the kids how to change the offense slightly to run right. The structure was the same and we could run the basic plays both ways. The kids were comfortable with running right as well as running left but left would remain our bread and butter offense. The kids decided with Dave and I to call this offense heavyset left to run left and heavyset right to run right. This kept it easy for the kids when we called the play in the huddle.

Along with this, we chose the kids to be the kickers from now on and started practicing the kicking game. We made a point of practicing the kicking game every practice from now on. Keeping in theme with "Practice makes perfect" I guess we were on our way. At this practice the coaches asked us to take some of the smaller kids on the team and show them the system. We agreed and took the little Warriors in to teach them smash face.

You have to understand here that we took half of the coaches big kids on defense to run this offense so the concerns expressed by the coaches at the time were valid concerns. We only had so many kids to work with this turned out to be a problem down the road. After running the offense with the smaller kids and as the other coach was running the defense with the big kids, the coach came over and asked Dave and I to run these kids on offense against the real defense. Dave and I agreed.

We set up and again the parents moved in to watch as the coaches set up the number 1 defense. I think now it was becoming a type of competition between the squads, kids and coaches. Dave the kids and I looked at it as a challenge if we could move our big kids with these smaller ones we could gain some credibility with all.

We got in the huddle, the first thing I did was reassure the new smaller kids and told them the older bigger ones would help them out and not to worry. All we asked is that they try as hard as they can. Well we called the play and ran the offense, It was slow against the bigger kids but we still picked up yards and I think the other coaches were getting frustrated with the formation. In the huddle, I would pump the kids and allow Justin to call the play the kids again created the rhythm and scored against their number one defense even with the small kids we could move the ball.

I think this really sold the coaches, it did not matter who ran the offense and it was so simple any one could be successful at it. The key was the quarterback, the lead blockers and one big kid in front on the line and this Dave and I kept as a constant. It was like a pocket of four kids if you kept these 4 players in tact the offense should run. I don't know how many people including the coaches and parents realized this or for that matter the kids, but Dave and I knew this and that's all that matter at this time. We ran the offense for a while and the coach then called practice.

The final night of practice came this week it was a fun week and the kids believed and felt good about themselves. We ran the same basic plays again and again all the time really pumping up the kids for tomorrow's big game. Dave and I had decided that the night before the games we had to really work on the mental conditioning of the kids. We practiced the kicking game and just tried to get prepared for our first debut and first win of the season, it was an exciting atmosphere for all.

Our opponents for tomorrow had the same disappointing record of 0 and 3 it was the battle of the Titans or the battle for the basement, whatever way you wanted to look at it. I looked at it as our first victory and our first step to redeeming these little Warriors. The coach called practice and then spoke for a while as the kids and parents gathered around. For the first time this season the coach turned to me and asked if I had anything to say to the kids.

I walked up to the kids and parents and smiled and said pump it up kids and bring it to me tomorrow because tomorrow we smash face with whoever gets in our way. I was beginning to get pumped already and the kids could sense it. I then screamed.

"Who are we?"

The kids screamed back, "The Warriors."

I then screamed. "What do we do?"

The kids were great they screamed back. "Smash Face, coach."

I thought to myself that was enough for the first pep rally. I told the kids bring it to me tomorrow bright and early. The coach then dismissed the kids and we the coaches gathered as we did. I could see some of the kids were pumped up as they headed to their parents and I thought, kids you have not seen anything yet, we will show it all tomorrow.

We talked and we reaffirmed that I was to go out on the field with the kids tomorrow and run the offense. I thanked the coaches for giving me the opportunity to run the field but I don't think either coach realized what they were getting into. I smiled and said to myself, hold on to your hats folks because the ride is about to begin.

After we went over the final strategies of the team, we broke up and Dave and I gathered the kids and headed home.

On the way home I talked with Jess and I began to pump him up, it's never to early to prepare right! As we were pumping up, I turned to Jess and said tomorrow, the Warriors will send a message to this league. The message is a simple one. "THE WARRORS ARE BACK".

I'd like to mention here that the Graham families contributions this week were two fold as Kim took it upon herself to set a cheerleading squad for the kids. She did an excellent job of it and all the other teams we were meeting had the little girls on the sidelines cheering on their teams and Kim felt it was time the Warriors had the same. I admired what Kim did it was great for the team, the kids and all involved. I think Kim, as well as the other parents felt the need for something Kim took the little daughters of the parents, the sisters of the players and organized the smallest cheerleading squad I had ever seen but they were sweet and I am sure were going to be a help. Thanks Kim, now the Warriors were complete.

"Game 4 of Season"

1st game after of our changes.

Record 0 win 3 defeats.

Now it seemed everything was in place and I for the first time this season felt truly prepared for a game. The sense of helplessness was now gone and I was confident with my kids. The only problem I had was I was nervous about my first coaching debut and my first time being on the field with the kids in a real game. I was wired all Friday night long after putting the boys down, I retired to my room to try to calm down a bit.

I finally settled myself down and told myself just go out and do what I know I can do. I found the most comforting thought was when I thought I have the kids and they believe in me and all I have to do is believe in them. It was ironic how the philosophy I tried to instill in the kids this week reversed its way to me and filled me with confidence. I chuckled and began to relax.

One thing still bothered me, Dave could not be at the game tomorrow so I was to go solo with the kids. I laughed at myself over the thought of sleeping this night away. I was so pumped up that I think I could have played the game right then.

Bzzzzzzzzzz 6:00 a.m. the clock went off and I jumped up out of bed and headed up stairs to greet the day. It was a beautiful morning for a game of football, I said aloud to myself. I can't explain how I felt it was like a mixture of nervous energy and anxiousness to get to the game and my pulse was racing. I went into poor Jess's room and I screamed at the top of my lungs.

"Are you ready for some football?"

Jess jumped up and looked at me, I yelled.

"Let's eat son, get dressed, pump it up and go smash face."

I then went into Kurt's room and did the same thing and about scared Kurt out of his skin.

I did not mean to be so crazy but I was just unbelievably wired. I think Jess knew, he had never seen me this bad before but he understood and knew that the intensity would be needed today. Kim woke up in all the noise and asked us to calm down and begged us to leave for the field. Kim knew better than to try to control us.

We left and piled into the van together I thought I have to get this madness out into the open air. The boys and I headed to the field all the while Jess and Kurt were going wild in the van.

In between all my screaming Jess piped up and told me that this field, our field of play today was his favorite field from last year. He told me he liked the Astroturf and was going to have a good game. I told Jess that was great and he had better be ready today. I was so zoned out I did not even notice how beautiful the morning was. We finally got to the field and I jumped out of the van, I just could not calm down. I got the kids to begin the pre-game ritual of walking the field. As we entered through the gates of the field, I thought to myself today's the day. The kids began to show up around 8:30 and as they entered the field I was screaming at the kids.

"Good Morning, time to wake up and play some football kids."

It was time for the kids and all to see exactly how wired we were to get to play this game.

All through the warm-ups, I was dancing around the kids and pumping them up and getting the kids zoned and ready for the game. Most of the kids were receiving well and were responding with their own screaming and this only fired me up more as the coaches approached the field. I remember one of the coaches came up to me and told me I had to calm down, I smiled at the coach and said.

"Sorry but I am calm and I'm ready for the game."

The coach just looked at me and walked away and I returned to the kids and the craziness.

It had got to a point that the coaches seemed to avoid me on the sidelines. I do believe that the head coach had thought he might have made a mistake after watching me. I kid you not if someone could of held me down long enough to plug me in I would of lit up the city. I created a frenzy that they all bought into, the kids were all running around and screaming like little lunatics not really making any sense just screaming and it was great.

This is when we began the zone playing in the zone controlled madness was all it was, after this game we named it the zone. It was our little place to meet before the games and our place to play the games. I looked over at the other team and they were all kind of looking at us.

To my pleasure and I'm sure everyone else's the two teams got on the field along with the refs and the game was about to begin. The coaches kept telling me to calm down and I kept replying that I was calm, all the while they were all avoiding me. I now look back at this morning and I laugh as I realize that I was nothing short of a raving lunatic.

The ball was kicked and our defense took to the field. I thought to myself at this moment the journey will now begin and our little secret between Jess and I had now taken flight. I remember I tried to go out on the field with the defense not realizing I was the offensive coach the coaches had to grab me and ask me to leave the field and wait my turn.

"ooooopppss I am calm, I am calm" I said to the coaches and returned to the sidelines.

The Warrior defense took control of the other team right away the opposing team could not move the ball against us and they kicked the ball back to us. It now was my turn on the field, the kids and I took to the field and we went into the huddle right away I looked at the kids and said.

"It's now time, we have to play and play hard, these other kids are not practicing with us, they want to knock us around like the other teams did. It's time to show everyone that no one is going to push us around anymore."

I then yelled. "Let's smash face."

I told Justin. "Call the play."

The kids lined up and as I watched I realized that I had worried so much of being in front of the crowd and being nervous that up until this moment I did not even realize the crowd or for that fact there was even a crowd woo hoo!

I was too wrapped up with the kids and the game to notice. I was soon to learn that you do not even notice the crowd when you got on the field, all you could see was the kids and the game thank God. Anyway the kids ran the play and it was mildly successful and we continued running the plays trying to create the rhythm for our kids. I kept pumping up the kids on the field so much that I thought the refs were going to give me a penalty for annoying them and the other kids.

The other team stopped us so we decided to kick the ball and pin the team deep for the defense and gain the field position. We did kick and pinned the team deep and our defense came out on the field. I was pleased with the kids, as they had done well their first time out. As we passed the defense to the sidelines I told the kids slap the defenses hands as you pass and tell them to go out there and play hard. The defense continued to dominate the other team's offense and held the team deep in their own end.

This went on back and forth for the first part of the game but we were slowly gaining the position on the other team and I could feel it coming.

SEAN GRAHAM

Our defense played well enough with the unbelievable play of Jess at the line backing spot.

I would like to say here that Jess single handily shut down about 70 percent of the other teams plays on his own. I was so proud of Jess and our defense, they kept the other team off balance long enough for our offense to get going. Jess seemed to be in the other teams backfield more than their own players I recall one of the parents from the sidelines was yelling somebody block number 9, my Jess.

Then it happened our defense scored a safety on the other team as a direct result of the field position the kids had created. The warriors lead 2-0. Well the kids were happy with the lead and the complete domination of this team. The team then kicked the ball back to us and we took to the field again. I got in the huddle with the kids and told the kids.

"We have to pump it up now, we have this team on its heels right now, let's put them all the way on their back."

I looked at Justin and said. "Come on son, start smashing that ball through the holes."

I looked at Kyle and Dan and told them, "Start opening up the holes for Justin, get angry and move these kids out of the way."

It took about 5 plays and a lot of emotion and our little Warriors pounded in their first offensive touchdown of the season and led this team 9-0. The kids went wild, I went wild, and so did the parents in the stand. It was a great monkey to get off our backs. It was as though the kids had just won the Super Bowl. I thought that this is new territory for these kids and it looked good.

After the celebrating, which I don't think the other people understood, as it was only a touch down but it was the Warriors first, and I believed the first of many to come. The game resumed and we went into half-time break, leading 9-0. The kids were higher than kites now so we kept the motivation going at half time we reassured the kids and congratulated them on their play.

The second half started and instead of going into every play the Warriors went onto defensively shutdown this team. As for my kids and I on offense, we pounded the ball into the end zone for another two touchdowns. As the kids got the rhythm of the game it was a sight to behold. The kids were patient, methodical and relentless, the other team couldn't stop our kids, they were like hungry wolves now that they could taste the win and I don't think there was anything to stop them now.

It was great to watch the little ones get their feet and their confidence about themselves. It was like night and day from the weeks previous. I kept teasing the kids in the huddle by asking them, who they were. I had meant it was as if they were a new team. However, the kids thought I meant, the pumping up chant and they kept replying to me.

"Warriors, coach."

I laughed at them, it was so sweet. The field and stands were electric now our kids were leading this team 23-0. The parents were cheering and chanting in the stands and Kim and the cheerleaders were leading the cheers on the sidelines. I looked over at the coach winked and smiled it felt like the whole field was alive with energy, positive energy and not only me this time.

I looked to the other teams sidelines and it was like they had just gone through a war. I could see the confusion and disarray in their coaches and kids. At one time on the field, the kids on the other team were almost crying every time they had to line up against our offense. On the field I remember the other teams coach was telling their kids to line up in front of where we were going to run and one of their kids said to the coach.

"You go there."

I kind of chuckled and thought it was time now to wind these kids down. We did not mean to humiliate anyone believe me, but our kids needed this today and now it was time to show some compassion. We slowed down the offense by experimenting a bit to have fun as the game was technically almost over, but in my eyes the game was over the second these Warriors got their confidence.

The game ended and the score was 23-0 and the kids had their first victory of the season. Yet more importantly they learned they could win at this game and compete. The parents on the sidelines were all jubilant and proud of their kids as they should be the kids played their hearts out today. They were all running around celebrating and it was a great moment for all. The kids went to shake hands with the other team which was the custom. I looked at our kids and stressed no taunting or teasing.

I told the kids we did not like it when it happened to us and I do not want us to do it to anyone else, it's not right. The kids were good about this the other coaches were telling the kids the same thing and this pleased me above all else. I wanted to teach these kids how to win but as well to be professional and mature and be good sports about it. I stressed to respect the other teams because we will someday meet them again and in all probability receive the same respect back from them in the future, this was important to me.

Well with all the celebrating going on and the parents now coming on to the field to congratulate their kids I thought it is a good time for me to slip away. I have to admit it was fun but emotionally draining. I was wiped, I couldn't really talk so I gathered up my stuff as the coach gathered the kids for the post game speech as he congratulated them with the parents standing there, I slipped away.

I met Kim on the field as she was headed over to the team. I looked at Kim and said.

"I got to go."

Kim understood and said she would get the boys and I could wait in the parking lot. I thanked Kim and headed out of the field to the van. I thought I was pushing a stroke here so when I got to the van I just stood there and tried to calm down from the high I was on wow. After a few minutes I heard someone calling my name, it was the coaches who were coming up to me. The coaches said.

"You were so pumped up you can't even hear us call you."

I explained. "I had to go and recharge the batteries and take it easy for a bit."

The coach laughed and said.

"I don't think you can calm down."

I could see the pleasure and excitement in the eyes of the coaches, they were still going on about the game and I told them I have to go home now and wind down a bit. Kim showed up with the boys and we piled in the van. We said good bye and we pulled away. I smiled and looked at Jess in the back of the van and said.

"What do you think son?" Jess smiled at me and said.

"It was amazing how well the team played." Kurt agreed.

The boys were saying, "We kicked butt Dad." I agreed. I told Jess.

"We now sent the message to the league, the Warriors are back and back big time." We all laughed and headed home happy. The Warriors were now 1-3 and on their way. I told the boys.

"We are out of the basement of the league now and more importantly we just gained back some respect for ourselves. You should be proud of yourselves."

When we got home we threw the tape of the game on we watched and we were all impressed with the kids and the team. It was a refreshing change to watch our team manhandle another team instead of being manhandled themselves. The kids looked like a professional ball team, they were so organized, and precise, I could not believe I was watching 6,7,8,9,10,and 11 year old kids. They executed the game plan to a tee, I was so proud of the kids.

The other thing that impressed me was the play of Jess on defense, as I mentioned earlier, Jess completely ruled the field from his middle linebacker spot. It was obvious the impact Jess had on the game watching the tape. I sat there and looked at Jess as we watched and thought to myself that this little guy gave everything today to help his Dad and his team. I cannot tell you how well he played you would have to be there to have seen it, but it was amazing. It was like one of those movies about a college team where one player decides that he is going to determine a game all by himself. That is exactly what Jess did in the first half. I told Jess.

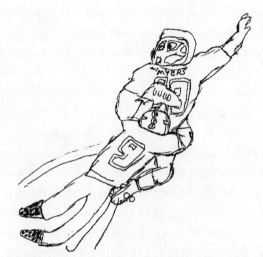

Jesse's spectacular sack (tackle)
Myers game

"You played an unbelievable game, son."

I thanked him with a hug for helping me out with my debut with his team. I looked at Jess, Kurt and Kyle as the tape ended and said.

"Now boys, that's football and that's smash face, all we have to do is keep smashing face from now on. We must believe and be ready from here on in for the rest of the season boys and then we will see what the playoffs bring."

The boys agreed as we rewound the tape for a second viewing. I watched the tape again with them and thought to myself, it was nice to see the boys happy with themselves. The kids were right it was time to savor this their first victory but next week it would be back to work, practice and to continue the journey we started. I thought for now enjoy it and relax, then get back at it Monday

On a personal note, I reflected on how much of an energy drain this was to me. I tried to figure out how I could find a happy medium to operate in.

Admittedly, I am an intense kind of guy when it comes to sports, especially when it involves my sons. Nevertheless, I had to figure out something or I was going to put myself in an early grave. This had just begun, there was going to be another 6 or 7 weeks of this. I decided if the kids could win again next week they would see that they could do it and I might be able to back off on the emotion a bit. The more the kids got confident the less energy I would have to exert. Therefore, I thought let us just take one game at a time.

Another personal note I would like to make here, was that for a league that doesn't emphasize winning the games as I was so repeatedly told, it was funny how one win could have such an affect on so many other people other than the kids.

I could see it in the coaches and the parents, and with all due respect, I do agree that winning at all costs is a poor attitude. Yet winning is a big part of the game whether we want to admit to ourselves or not.

I asked the kids what they wanted when we started this journey and they told me they wanted to win and after all it is the kids who play the game not us. This is my own opinion on this issue and it might be wrong for me to express this, but I think the thrill of competition is what makes any sport have life. As well as having the courage to go out and face the threat of defeat along with savor the glory of victory.

The weekend rolled along and I mulled over in my mind what had happened and realized how right Dave was about the basics and repetition. I then phoned Dave to let him know what happened, Dave told me he knew what happened by the way his son Gregory was acting when his mom brought Greg home from the game. Dave told me.

"Greg was still excited and wired from the game hours later."

I laughed I told Dave, "The plan worked and worked well, the kids eliminated the mistakes had ball control and great field position all game."

Dave was happy that our strategy had worked. Dave told me he knew the kids would win if we stuck with the plan. The only thing that Dave was surprised with was that the kids had not scored more than 23 points. We congratulated ourselves and I got off the phone. I thought to myself that this game might have been luck and with all due respect, the other team did have a 0-3 record as well.

I did not get the impression that the other team was weak, they seemed to play hard their kids were bigger than ours and they seemed like a good team. But our kids on defense wouldn't let them get on track and when our offense was on the field we controlled the ball so long the other team really never had a chance to get their rhythm.

I decided that time would tell if it was luck or not and I went about my weekend.

Practice on Monday night, the boys were still excited and so was I. We wanted to get to the tiny practice field and see the kids and talk about the big game, no doubt in detail. I was not sure what to expect from the coaches and the parents. The kids I think knew would be excited, I really did not worry about them all that much. I think now we were developing a bond between us. The little park seemed different tonight as the boys and I walked in. Some of the parents were there with their kids and this was somewhat odd as we usual got there early, I took it as a good sign. I walked up to the coach, handed him the tape of the game and smiled and said.

"It's good."

I could feel the sense of approval from the coaches as well as the parents that were there. I thought to myself the difference in the little park tonight

I think was the wind of change had blown threw and the atmosphere here was one of positive energy. I gave the coach my analysis of the game and the kids as well what I thought would be the keys to work on this week in practice the coach smiled and agreed. Dave joined us and we all discussed the game and the upcoming week. I could sense from Dave and the coaches that Saturdays game was a good thing but let's not get out of hand here, 1 game does not make a season. I agreed with the thought process but I thought hey these kids are good and now they know it.

I admired how the coaches were handling the changes so far the coaches kept perspective and the attitude of lets continue with the work and practice was the mandate. I felt that we should let the kids get more involved in the strategies and the overall structure of the team as they were the team. I thought let's stop dictating to these kids and let them lead us through the offense and defense. I think what I wanted was a more hands on approach from the kids and for them to take some ownership of their team.

Anyway practice started and the kids jumped in. The kickers began to practice as we had asked them to do every night. The kicking game needed to be worked on. The kids continued the repetition and were now kind of blowing away the kids on defense in practice. The kicking game we now practiced at every chance, it was coming along and coming late into the fall and the cold weather this would affect the outcomes of the games. The kicking game would become increasingly important now for field position.

The other coach had some suggestions and new plays to incorporate in the new offense and both Dave and I thought lets not confuse the kids. They are doing good now lets go slow with them. It all boiled down to two gravely different coaching philosophies and styles. We found that these coaches liked the bang one time big play wide open offense. Dave and I felt at this level and age basic blocking and running and ball control offense was what was needed. Dave and I found that a lot of our time was spent convincing people of this philosophy, we just had to be patient with it and allow the kids to operate it.

I think I could feel the pull and struggle that Dave and I were going to have with these coaches. This bothered me because I thought the deal was we run the offense and this is what we were trying to do and it was becoming obvious to me we were going to have problems doing this. The one thing I was thankful for was I think the kids believed in us now and that was all I really needed.

The week plodded along and practice went fine. I recall the night that the defense coach asked Kurt to mark off the line of scrimmage in practice and call it out. This meant as the defense lined up on the ball for the play, one of the kids would stretch their little legs to measure a yard distance and after the kid did this he would yell out. "One yard." Then the kid would yell out. "Take A Knee" to the other kids on defense. Well Kurt was asked to do this and do it Kurt did with all the hustle and bustle of the practice going on.

Kurt caught not only his defense's attention but also everyone within a 10 mile radius. Dave and I were at the other end of the field and all you could hear was this cracking and screeching voice. "ONE YARD TAKE A KNEE." It was comical, the smallest kid on the squad ordering all the bigger kids around.

As Dave and I walked up to watch, Kurt would swat the kids who did not take a knee or verbally berate them until they listened to him.

"Kurt took his job serious." I chuckled and told Dave." Just like the old man."

Amongst all this, the coach came to me and told me the team we faced this week had the same record 1-3 but they were a much bigger team and more physical than the team we just faced. The coach seemed worried about this team again. Dave and I tried to assure the coach not to worry this was when I first told the coach the kids were not going to lose anymore. The kids now knew how to win and that was exactly what the kids were going to do.

I don't think the coaches believed me, I think they thought that I was a bit cocky but I knew the kids believed this and that's all that mattered to me. I began to explain to the kids that the newfound madness was to be called the zone from now on. This zone was to be the little place in our heads where we would meet collectively for our games together. I made it like a game to the kids it was like our little secret place and in that little place we were invincible together. Nothing could harm us and the rest of the world outside the zone did not exist to us.

In practice I would grab the kids and tell them look into my eyes now. Focus on what your doing and what we're asking of you, think only of what you're doing, focus, find the zone and find that little spot. It was so sweet to watch their eyes cue in. All I was asking for was complete concentration and commitment to me as well as their teammates. The kids to my delight understood this quite easily.

I would tell them, think and get your heads into the zone, then I would confirm with the little Tykes. I would ask them where are you right now and the kids would reply in the zone coach as the kids would reply they would also point to their heads to physically let me know where they were. I felt that the kids now had a good understanding of the mental aspect of the game. How important it was to be mentally prepared as well as, physically prepared. The buzzwords at practice quickly became the zone, think, concentrate, focus and smash face. I felt this was just as important as the physical aspects and possible more so.

On Thursday night of this week I was sitting at home with Jess after practice and we were watching one of the tapes of the games. Jess put on his helmet and we were playing around. I noticed some Halloween make-up on the table as we were nearing this holiday. I stopped and thought for a minute. I said to myself when the idea came clear to me "no Sean don't do it" but I couldn't help myself I had to see how it would look. I told Jess to take his helmet off and he did.

I then convinced Jess of my idea. Poor kid, I took the make-up and seeing as his team was called the Warriors, I figured lets give them some war paint why not go all the way. I painted on Jess's face my personal impression of what I thought war paint would look like. Well it looked good and intimidating. I used black and red and just smeared it all over his face. It resembled the movies I had watched of Indian warriors. Some research, eh! After we applied the paint I told Jess.

"Go look at yourself in the mirror." and as he ran to the mirror I said.

"Put your helmet on first son."

Jess came back and told me, "I like it Dad."

I laughed and told him to growl and come at me like he was in a game and Jess did.

"You look so scary." I said.

I called Kurt to come see, Jess growled at Kurt and Kurt told us he liked it too. Now it was the big test, we called Mom out to see. Kim came out and I told her to watch the wild middle linebacker coming at her. Jess growled as he rushed Kim I looked at Kim and said.

"What do you think?"

Well Kim gave me a look that said it all. The look was one of are you nuts Sean. I laughed for I had come to learn Kim was one of those people that you always do the opposite of when you want to be wacky and wild.

Kim's look in essence sold me on the new tactic, thanks, once again, Kim.

I told Jess. "Tomorrow at practice son we will paint your face up and we won't say anything to anyone and just see what the response is."

Jess agreed. We painted up Jess's face on Friday night. On the way to practice I was laughing in the van as I was thinking about how everybody would like the idea. It was then that I noticed that Jess was taking this war paint thing serious. He looked so intense in the back of the van I thought wow this might not be as ridiculous as I originally thought.

It was the final night of practice before the game we arrived at the park and Jess ran out to the kids as I headed to the coaches to talk. I cannot remember which kid came first to me and asked for some of the paint but before I knew it the kids were all lined up at me now screaming for the war paint. It was something the coaches and the parents were all wondering what was going on. The coaches looked at me confused, so I called Jess over to us as Jess got to us I told him to take off his helmet and he did. The coach looked at me as if I had lost whatever faculty I had. I smiled at the coach and I told the coach.

"The kids are Warriors and now they will have the war paint, and the games from now on are not games but wars."

The coach looked at me in disbelief said, "Well okay Sean."

The kids were all lined up now asking for the paint, so I pulled the paint kit out of my pocket and began to apply it to the kids faces one at a time. I then turned it into a ritual I began to tell the kids.

"War paint was a sign of courage for the warrior, the paint this week is free but tomorrow they had to earn the right to wear the paint."

In the game tomorrow the kids had to prove to the spirits that they had the courage and bravery to be able to wear war paint. The kids agreed. I then told them.

"This is not a game. In order to be a warrior you have to be strong and brave and from now on we will declare war on whoever gets in front of us."

The kids loved it and I began to think I'm becoming a bigger kid than they are and enjoying it. I thought what the hell if it works and it was kind of fun, I think that even Dave along with the other coaches thought I was losing it.

Practice went on that night and the coach called it early this night. He called the kids in for the speech before the game. The kids and the parents moved in and I could see that the parents were looking at the war paint on their faces. I laughed to myself, the coach made a good speech and asked the other coaches to speak if we had something to say. Dave and the other coach went up and talked to the kids and parents. Then came my turn I got in front of them and all I said rather loudly was.

"WHO ARE WE?" The kids replied.

"WARRIORS." I then yelled.

"WHAT DO WE DO?" The kids replied.

"SMASH FACE." Then I added.

"Start pumping it up kids and start finding the zone now and bring it to me tomorrow. "I then asked.

"What are you going to bring to me tomorrow?" The kids all replied.

"The zone coach."

Then we had a group chant and the coach then dismissed the kids.

The kids headed out the coaches would gather by the van and we would go over the game plan for tomorrow. I would have to tell the coaches again not to worry the kids were in the zone and they were going to win the game. We had to start having confidence in our kids and not worry about the other teams. I heard so much about the other teams how big they were and how good and the coaches were usually right about this but I wanted to talk more about our kids and stop worrying about the other teams so much and start believing that our kids can beat these teams. I guess just being more confident, I tried to express this to the coaches but I usually just said.

"Don't worry about it." and kept it to myself.

The meeting of the coaches ended and I gathered up Jess, Kurt and headed home. I smiled at Jess and asked if he was ready for tomorrow and he smiled and said,

"Oh yea."

We got home and tried to settle in for the night awaiting the morning's light.

"Game 5 of Season"

2nd game after our change.

Record 1 win 3 defeats.

Buzzzzzzzzzzzzzzzzzzzzzzzzzzzzzz it was 6:00 a.m. and as usual I was flying up the stairs. I made my coffee as I watched the 3 boys sleeping on the living room floor. It was the Friday night ritual of videos and camping out in the living room. Kim usually could not last with the kids and she would find her way into one of their rooms and flake out. It was so peaceful I looked out the window and saw that the morning was overcast and I could smell rain. It was a cool damp fall morning and the weather station was calling for heavy rain the night before. I chuckled and thought great football weather, I turned and watched the boys and thought how beautiful they were in their slumber. I thought how peaceful. Well enough of that, I started the screaming and dancing as I awoke the boys.

"Are You Ready for some football. A Saturday morning party."

I would sing this over and over again it was my version of the Monday night football's theme song. I noticed Jake in his sleepy stupor look at me, get up and head into his room to find his mom and some sanctuary. As he entered his room and shut the door, I told Jess and Kurt that Jake just did not understand yet but he would in time. I fed the boys all the while pumping them up and screaming, Jess went into his quiet mode. Kurt was still one of the young kids on the team and would take a bit of time to understand the madness as he just gave me that stare.

After the kids ate we dressed and applied the war paint for the first game. Jess and Kurt loved the war paint and as I applied the paint, I reminded them that they had to earn the right to wear this paint today. The courage of the warrior was to come out along with this paint. I thought I will have to let Dave know of this new ritual this morning as we greet the kids and apply the paint. After all this was done we woke up Jake and Kim and headed out the door.

We piled in the van and headed over to Kyle's place as he lived close and we would drive him to the field with us. We applied the paint to Kyle's face as we headed to our home field. When we got to the field as usual we were the first there. I told them to get out and begin walking the field as the kids and I walked the morning was slowly breaking. As I said, rain was in the air but the field was clear and quiet kind of like a natural little haven nestled in the woods behind the community high school. I thought I am proud to call this home. The field really had character much the same as the character of the kids. As we walked Dave showed up with his son and the other kids began arriving to the field. The other team's parents and kids began to slowly trickle in. I told Dave about the rituals with the war paint and he agreed. As the kids began to arrive I watched and went up to each kid and greeted them with a bellowing.

"GOOD MORNING" "Are you ready for some football?"

I would then go up to each kid and grab them by the helmets and tell them to look into my eyes. As the kids looked, I began to tell each one of them that it was time to reclaim our home field. No more allowing other teams to come in our backyard and push us around that was over as of today. I then told each one to walk to the end of the field from one goal post to the other, at each end of the field and introduce themselves to the goal posts and the field. Let the field know that we are here today to defend and protect our home. Some of the kids did not know what to think but none questioned me and all did what I asked. It was cute to watch them all walk the field and talk to the posts. After this Dave began to warm-up the kids in their squads and I just walked threw their ranks screaming.

"WHO ARE WE?" The kids would reply.

"THE WARRIORS." I would go on.

"WHAT DO WE DO?" The kids would reply.

"SMASH FACE." I would then scream.

"I CAN'T HEAR YOU." This would go on back and forth as Dave warmed them up. I loved this time before the game as I would walk around and try to take a moment for each kid and smile and wink and say are you ready and see where their eyes were. I would further ask the kids to start focusing in, find the zone and get ready to concentrate kids on what we have to do here. As I walked, I chuckled as I saw all the little faces waking up and focusing in and the war paint, the new found motivator.

As we were prepping the kids the other team was in full practice at the other end of the field. I looked down and thought God these kids look bigger and meaner than the kids last week. I thought where do they find these kids. The parents were all gathering and the field was now awake to the bustle of the pre game warm ups and the gathering of the fans. The coaches arrived and I reported to the coaches as Dave ran some drills with the kids. The defensive coach went out on the field and took over the drills from Dave. The refs arrived and set up and the game was about to begin.

We won the coin toss and asked to receive first so the other team kicked to us and the game began. Along with the beginning of the game the rain came. The field already was muddy and wet from the rain the night before and now it was going to get worse for the kids and their footing. I took to the field with the kids for our first offensive drive. I got in the huddle with the kids and said. "All right now Justin call the play and kids lets start some SMASH FACE." Justin called the play and the kids lined up as I watched the kids from behind I saw this huge kid on the other team. He was almost as big as I was and the sad part was that they had positioned this kid right where we run. I thought it is going to be tough on the kids today. We ran a few plays and our kids were successful in picking up a few yards, not a lot but we were moving the other team a bit. We picked up our first down and I was impressed in the huddle. I told the kids.

"Your doing great, lets stay together and keep moving these kids."

The drive was slow but successful, we got another first down and we were controlling the ball again, I was happy. We came up to second down and about 6 yards to go. I got the kids in the huddle and I told the kids.

"We are going to change the play a bit here, everything will be the same for everyone other than Justin and Avi."

I looked at Justin and said.

"I want you to hand the ball off to Avi and Avi, I want you to run outside instead of inside."

I smiled at Avi and said.

"Son, when Justin gives you the ball you run like the devil and don't stop." Avi smiled and said.

"Okay Coach."

Avi Slack was about the smallest kid on our team and had great speed and confidence. I thought if he could get outside with his speed he could break it. I explained this to the kids in the huddle and the kids agreed. I also thought as I had told the kids before that Avi was so small the other team probably would not see him until it was too late. So we all agreed in the huddle, Justin called the play and the kids lined up I stood back and watched. Well the kids ran the play perfectly and as I suspected I don't think the other team could see Avi.

As he turned the corner and scampered 36 yards up the field untouched, for the first touchdown of the game. The Warriors lead 6-0 early. It was a great. Even better was Avi's run back to his teammates and our sidelines he tore up the field with his arms high up in the air and his eyeballs looked like silver dollars as he tore past me. The parents were celebrating the kids and it was good. I think we rather shocked the other team by scoring so quickly. After all the celebrating and the excitement, we kicked the ball to the other team and it was the defenses turn to take the field.

The game became really bogged down for the rest of the first half neither team could move the ball, it turned into a real dogfight now with the rain falling and the mud everywhere. We kept pumping the kids up. However, you have to understand the other team had a similar record as ours and this game would determine the playoff fate of both teams. The winner would possibly go to the B round and the loser in all probability would go to the C round. We knew this and I am sure the other team knew this too. It was obvious the way the kids were playing each other neither would give an inch. It was exciting and intense.

The first half ended with the Warriors leading 6-0. Dave took the kids into the end zone for his half time motivational speech as I talked with the coaches.

Dave's speeches were great as the kids always came back ready and eager to go. The Coaches and I talked and I told the coach that there was one hell of a battle of wills going on out there, he agreed. We also agreed that the game had turned into a drag down street fight. I told the coach we were going to keep it simple we have the lead and we want no mistakes as I thought a mistake might be a killer in this type of game.

Back to the game or the mud bowl, the two teams were still struggling with each other. It was like two prizefighters fighting it out and neither willing to hit the mate. We had the lead I thought we would play it safe and try to kill this game and win 6-0. Just as I was thinking this we were forced into a 3rd down and long deep in our end. The other team was slowly gaining position on us, and I think mostly because of the size difference.

Anyway, we decided to kick as we snapped the ball one of the other teams kids jumped offside and hit Kyle hard as Kyle tried to kick. Kyle was injured on the play and had to leave the field. We were in trouble as Dan was our back up kicker and he was hurt earlier. As I mentioned earlier this was a tough game and we now had no kicker. We had to kick from deep in our end and the 3rd quarter was now ending, we were in trouble. I looked at little Katherine and asked her to kick the ball. She had shown an interest in kicking at practice and had shown me the heart and the spirit to do what was asked of her.

Katherine was a real trooper, I smiled at her in the huddle and told her not to worry and just kick the ball, I told her she could do it and she knew she could do it. We ran the play and Katherine was great, she stood in there just as I knew she would. Confidently she tried to kick the ball but the same kid who had jumped off side earlier did it again and hit Katherine as she tried to get the kick off. We turned the ball over deep in our end as this kid was not called for the penalty and I was angry with the ref. I told the ref someone is going to get hurt here as this team in my opinion was doing this all game.

Anyway we tried and the defense had to take to the field and try to hold this team that now had the momentum. I stormed to the sidelines as I was still angry at the ref and the coach came over to me to calm me down. I was thankful that at least Katherine did not get hurt. Kicking is a dangerous job on a fair play let alone on an offside twice in a row, I thought what bad luck. The other team's offense took to the field deep in our end, and we all cheered on our defense. The other team was too close and eventually pounded the ball in for their first touchdown and we were all tied up at 6-6.

The other team had to try for the point and if good they would take the lead with the game winding down now. The defense stood tall and broke up the other teams play for the single point, we were tied now and we were getting the ball back. We received the ball after the other team celebrated their score and I went out on the field with the kids. I will never forget this huddle. I started talking to the kids and it was like we had lost all steam and we were being lulled to sleep. As I talked with the kids Danny looked at me in the huddle and said.

"Hey coach, we got to start screaming and growling here, we have to move these kids out of the way, right?"

I looked at Dan and smiled and thank God, he still had the fire in him. Well, Dan started growling and so did the rest of the kids in the huddle and so did I. We woke up and I told Justin to call the play. Then I said to the kids.

"Get angry and take back the lead." It was great as the kids lined up I began screaming.

"Come on kids get it up, start growling."

The referees the other team and the coaches were all looking in amazement. Dan and Kyle our two lead blockers were beginning to scream out loud like animals I'm sure everyone on the sidelines were wondering what was going on you could hear these kids all through the park. The kids ran the play and blew the other kids off the line. We were back, while in the huddle we were all chanting, growling and screaming now. It must have resembled some kind of feeding frenzy. The kids lined up again and I could see now that some of the kids on the other team were getting scared, I could see it in their eyes.

The kids smashed through the other team again and now the parents were getting into it on the sidelines, they were cheering the kids were screaming I was pumping. The field was alive with the energy, the frenzy had begun and again the kids smashed the ball all the way down to the other teams 5 yard line. We tried on third and goal and did not make it, we were smoking now but the other team made a great play and stopped us on the two-yard line. We turned the ball over to the other team with only a few minutes to go now. I congratulated the kids as we left the field to the defense and we were satisfied now to tie the game and have it end that way. The kids did good and I was proud of them.

As I was talking to the coach on the sidelines I heard a great cheer come from the parents on the sidelines. I turned to see one of our little Warriors on defense had the football, as he ran towards our bench with it and the rest of the kids on the field were all celebrating. I looked at the coach and screamed, "Fumble."

I ran out on the field and sure enough the other team fumbled on its first play and turned the ball over to us on their 3 yard line.

I was crazy I was running hugging every Warrior I could find as the coach was screaming out behind me offense on the field. We got in the huddle and I told the kids.

"Let's do it and lets do it now, Justin call the play and let's smash face."

The kids lined up and smashed the ball into the end zone for the go ahead touchdown. It was unbelievable the kids were going wild. The parents were all cheering and the Warriors lead 12-6 and the game almost over.

What a hard fought battle, I felt bad for the other team it was a tough way to lose such a good game. We attempted to kick the point after and again were unsuccessful, I thought if this was our bread and butter play we would all starve. After the failed point we kicked the ball back to the other team there were 3 plays remaining. How wonderful the turn of events were, with the fumble and it all happened in front of the corner of the field the parents were standing at.

As the ball sailed downfield the Warriors were all wired they ran down after the ball and as the other team touched the ball again the ball came free and it was another fumble. The Warriors had recovered the ball again. Everybody who had finished cheering the last set of events began the cheering all over again as the Warrior kids were running around wildly with the ball. We had the ball near the other teams end zone and I am sure the kids would have scored again if we had given them the chance as I headed out to the field with the kids. The coach gave me a gesture to take a knee. I nodded but as I got up to the huddle and the kids were all chanting as they waited for me Justin the quarterback looked at me and said.

"Coach why don't we just take a knee for three plays."

I thought, what a wonderful idea we got in the huddle and I told the kids that Justin was calling the play. Justin and I explained to the kids that this was the way to end a game like this instead of trying to rub the other teams nose in the loss. We show some sportsmanship by saying we won and it was a tough battle and that we think the other team was a formidable foe this day. I told Justin to run the play, as I stood back and watched, the kids ran all three plays without me, it was great.

The kids ran the 3 plays and the parents gave a constant standing ovation from the sidelines. I was so proud of the kids. Every opportunity we had we tried to instill compassion and respect. When playing this game the kids on the other team were visibly upset over the loss and I am sure the coaches on the other team appreciated the gesture by our kids.

The ref blew the whistle and the game was over, Warriors 12-6 victors wow the kids had just won two games in a row and more importantly they claimed back their home field. The kids were all celebrating along with the parents and coaches. After the kids shook hands with the other team, the coaches brought out the cokes and the coach had his post game speech.

I remember that he had talked about how proud he was of the team and its effort in the last two weeks. I think the kids needed to hear this from the coach it was a great two games, the kids were smoking now and they were proud of themselves and so was everyone else. I think that what was most important was that the kids now saw for themselves that they could win a game. If they put their minds and hearts into it and learned to play as a unit one unit, not three or four but one. I shook Dave's hand and congratulated him as well as the other coaches. The rain had stopped now all were gathered and the atmosphere around was now much improved in my opinion.

The kids began to break up and head home Dave, the coaches and I gathered at the van for a few minutes. As we talked the coach told us we were probably in the B round of the playoffs, not bad for a team that was expected to win only one game this season. I told the coach, I furthered said.

"Getting to the playoffs is one thing what we do in the playoffs is what matters." The coach agreed.

We talked a bit more and then we broke up. As I remember all I wanted to do was get home get in some dry clothes and watch the tape of this great struggle we just fought. I gathered the kids and headed home. Jess and Kurt were happy and pleased with themselves as we drove home, we talked about the game and we were all still very excited.

When we got home, we changed and sat down and watched the tape together. Kim was impressed with the kids and the team. As we watched the tape she told us that she was happy for them and the poor little cheerleaders who got soaked this day but stuck it out. We saw this one play made on defense and it was Kurt. I must have missed this play thank God for the tapes. The other team was running the ball outside, and who else but little Kurt with all his speed, ran the play down as he got to the kid who was carrying the ball. Kurt just flung himself on the kid's back and held on for dear life, the kid was so big he dragged Kurt down the field with Kurt's legs dangling in the wind. The finishing touch on the play came when Jess came flying through the crowd and just smacked the kid off his feet. I began to laugh and chant at the boys, the Graham boys making the play.

The boys laughed we ran the play again and again. As the tape ended I looked at the boys and told them how proud of them I was and how they were now looking like a football team and they should be proud of themselves.

Two brother making a tackle
(Belcir Game)

Kyle, Jess, and Kurt went about their weekend and I watched the tape again on my own. I reflected on the aspect of the kids playing as a team. At one time there was 3 or 4 clicks on this team and nobody seemed to get along at all. The ones who seemed to be the bullies and the aggravators were now taking on the roles of protectors and guardians of the smaller kids that they had once bullied.

With or without the winning this was a victory in itself, the games were just a bonus watching the kids grow and learn about each other was the gratifying part to me. How marvelous change can be when change is welcomed and excepted. How intelligent and mature this rag tag bunch of misfits were becoming right before our eyes. I chuckled to myself and thought, enjoy this Sean, for this type of thing does not happen often enough in our life times. I awaited next week's practice.

Monday night came, as the boys ran off to muck it up with the other kids I walked over to the coaches and handed the tape of the game and we began to talk. As we were discussing the game the head coach began to explain to me that as a result of the win on Saturday the Warriors were now in the B round of the playoffs.

I asked the coach if he was sure and he told me he checked into it and it did not matter what happened this week the kids were in the B round. This bothered me right away. We had one more game to play to end the season. Whether it mattered or not to the standings or the coaches, it was insignificant to me and it mattered to the kids. I tried to express my concerns to the coach about taking a relaxed attitude towards a game that was insignificant in the standings. He seemed to understand my concerns but I did not think he was being very sincere with me. It seemed he was satisfied to be in the B round and this game was a nothing game.

I held my tongue and went along with the strategy that was being discussed for this week's practice. Part of this strategy was the coaches new plays on offense. When I heard this I thought the kids have just won their last two games with this offense, lets just leave it alone. I did agree in essence with the coach, that we should open up the offense a bit in the event that some team should be able to stop our offense. Then I was told, we should teach the kids the game of football.

I'd like to say here that after I heard this comment I had a hard time trying to figure out what game it was that Dave and I were teaching these kids over the last 3 weeks.

I did resent this comment but I for the life of me tried to understand and I realized that Dave and I had to work through this for the kids. It was not a time for egos for either me or the other coaches. I told the coach I would appreciate it if we did not tell the kids that this game meant nothing to us. I felt that we cannot let up right now with the kids, they have found something and they are happy with it and successful with it. My personal feelings were that if we began to change things now we were asking for trouble.

Nevertheless, he was the head coach it was his team and I had to respect that. I waited for Dave to show up to discuss the newfound life in the coaches, as I did the coaches began practice. Soon Dave arrived and we talked as the coach began to introduce his new plays to the kids on offense.

Dave was of the same thought as I Dave thought leave the offense alone it works and its simple and the kids were comfortable with it. You have to understand that Dave was a lot more forceful with the coaches than I was. Dave took a very simple and logical look at things and this characteristic of Dave was one of the biggest reasons this system worked. He tried to voice his opinion to the coach, but it seemed that the coach was rejuvenated now after his burn out earlier this season and was serious about opening things up. So Dave and I decided to let the coach do his thing and we would still run the offense the way it should run. We decided to let the coach practice with the kids his plays and when we got the kids, we would just stick to the basic offense whether he liked it or not.

I know now that I'm beginning to get into the politics of the game a bit but I felt I had to as this week's game had what I felt a profound affect on the kids and the team. Anyway I think what happened here this week was a clash of philosophies, both his and ours. The feeling at the tiny park was one of pleasure and hope as the parents and the kids were basking in this newfound success. The parents and their kids were now looking confident and proud and began to resemble a tight nit football team and family. As the coach practiced his new plays on offense Dave and I made sure the first plays to be practiced each night were the basic ones.

One of the kids this week came to me and told me that he was getting confused with the offense because of the new plays. I trusted and had great respect for this kid, so I took him aside and asked him to bear with us and trust me because when it came game time their was only one offense to run and that was smash face. The kid smiled and said.

"All right, coach."

I was later to learn from this kid's mother that he had went home crying after practice because of the confusion. I know the head coach meant no harm to the kids or the team, but the confusion was there and the frustration for the kids. I think that we forgot about them and what they thought. It was a bit of a mental battle going on and I am sure the kids sensed it. I am equally sure that it distracted them as well as us.

I can now say that this was personal to me, this team and my sons and this journey with these kids I took very seriously whether that is right or wrong. I really didn't want any interference on the goal the kids Dave and my son had set out on.

On a lighter note here I would like to talk about Katherine here our tough, pro-bowl like corner back. She was on defense in practice and I kept walking around her and teasing her. I kept saying to her, so they call you a corner back in this league, I would then chuckle at her. This went on for about two or three plays. Well for the fourth time I said it as I brushed up against her and used my weight to nudge her over, as I walked away I was saying.

"I laugh at you as a cornerback."

Just as I finished the words, whack I dropped to my knees like a rock. Katherine was fed up with me and took me down at my knees hard. I turned and looked at her and all she did was growl at me with such a show of emotion. I smiled and said.

"Atta girl Kath, don't take shit from anyone."

I patted her on the shoulders and walked away.

I would do this as much as possible when the coach was practicing defense. As most of my kids on offense were part of defense, I used to walk through the defense as they set up and practiced. I would tease the kids and try to get them angry with me. I remember one time in practice I began to bump each kid as they lined up for scrimmage. I would walk through them as the other coaches ran the drills and as I walked through, I would nudge them with my weight. The kid's that I would nudge would give me the look and the stare, but I think that out of respect they would not hit me or retaliate. I thought that I have to get through to these kids that no matter who it was nobody was allowed to mess with the Warriors.

Well it finally happened, it was Jess who I hit in practice and he was fed up. I was becoming annoying now, anyway I hit Jess and insulted his defense as I walked away Jess hit me from behind and kept hitting me. As I pushed Jess away the rest of the Warriors came to Jess's defense. I found myself trying to fend off a hoard of heathens and I loved it. After I got myself back on my feet and collected I looked at the kids and told them its about time someone responded to me.

I told the kids that it took awhile but no matter who it is I don't want you kids to allow anyone to disrespect any of you. If some one does, I want all of you to be in that persons face. The kids just looked at me in their intense fashion and I told them.

"Don't forget this, nobody messes with the Warriors, if you mess with one you mess with all."

I wanted to mention this as these were some of the beliefs I tried to instill in these kids to take care of each other no matter who or what especially on the field in the game. I used to tell these kids against the wishes of the other coaches, that if the kids saw someone on the other teams taking advantage of or bullying one of the Warriors in a game that the Warriors would gladly take the penalty as the result of a retaliation hit. I remember I was told so many times not to teach our kids this but our kids were small and if someone wanted to take advantage of that the kids were not going to accept it. The bottom line with the kids and I was that we would play clean and be professional but we were not going to take anyone's intimidation no matter what.

We eventually got through the week of practice and the coach called the kids in on the final night of practice and made his little speech and after he was done, the coach allowed the rest of the coaches the chance to speak. When it came my turn to speak, I tried to pump-up the kids but I just did not feel the same, it was like I was lost but I did not want the kids to see this. So we did the Warrior chant and the smash face chant but it just was not the same as the previous weeks. Practice ended and the coach dismissed the team and again the coaches gathered to discuss the game strategies.

I once again tried to emphasize my concerns about thinking this game meant nothing to the team, the coach agreed but I think he felt the opposite of what he was saying to me. We broke up and headed home. In the parking lot I talked with Dave about the new plays and the relaxed attitude. Dave just simply said.

"Sean you're on the field with the kids, run the offense the kids know and just ignore the coaches when they ask for the changes."

I told Dave.

"This would be tough to do."

Dave replied.

"Well you have been doing a great job of it, so far" and then laughed.

He mentioned.

"Just do what you know the kids can do."

After this we headed home and on the way I talked with Jess and asked him how he felt about the changes. Jess said straight out to me.

"Dad, do what you do best and don't listen to anyone please."

He also continued on to say that the new offense was confusing and he told me most of the kids on offense felt the same way. I thanked Jess and he repeated.

"Dad don't listen to anybody we're doing good now." I smiled and said.

"Don't worry, Jess."

We got home and the boys were setting up with their videos for the evening. I retired to my room and tried to sort out these feelings of insecurity that I had.

Kim came in the room, we began to talk and I told Kim that I do not feel very confident about tomorrow's game. I told her that I was not sure why but I just do not feel strong at all. Kim got angry with me and said.

"Sean just have confidence in your kids, you are telling everyone else to have confidence in the kids, you do the same."

She then further stated. "The kids respect you and will do anything you ask them to do, so on the field tomorrow just be with the kids and trust them as they trust you."

She was right, I stopped and thought for a moment, and she made so much sense to me. I thought I have the kids on the field and that is all I need. I thought it was almost now like the kids and I were feeding off each other when it came to confidence and the will to do what we were doing. I thanked Kim for her words of wisdom and she left me to relax and get some rest. I was still feeling intimidated about something but thanks to mom not as much.

"6th and final game of regular season"

3rd game after change.

2 wins, 3 defeats.

Bzzzzzzzzzzz, Yahoo round three the buzzard woke me up and as usual, I flew up the stairs. I made my coffee and sat down to focus in before I disturbed their slumber.

I looked out the window and saw that it was another beautiful fall morning. The sun was bright and everything was dry the birds were chirping in the apple tree on the lawn, our garden was flourishing and it was all so pretty and serene. I thought today we would end the season with a bang and we will take these kids to a record of 3-3 on the season after today's victory and then head into the playoffs. Today's game was against a team that had a 4-1record and was of the elite in this league. The last time we met this team was the third game of the season which was when the coach turned the offensive over to me and this team thrashed our kids on our field that day. It was time for justice today and payback. I went to the bathroom, looked in the mirror smiled at myself and said.

"Welcome back Sean."

Those feelings of intimidation were gone and the lunatic looking in the mirror was ready to pump it up again. I headed into the living room and began the screaming and the chanting to wake the boys. The boys got up and we began the madness, as mentioned earlier the morning was outstanding. I thought to myself, it doesn't get any better than this. The field we walked out on to was beautiful it was well groomed and well maintained. The kids began to walk the field as did I as the kids began to arrive to the usual bellowing of good morning are you ready we began the warm-ups.

Dave set the kids up and began the exercises as I roamed through the rows of the kids chanting, smiling and winking at them as their little faces woke up. I thought these kids must think I'm nuts. I laughed and thought they should talk to Jess and Kurt, these boys live with the madness. Anyway the coaches arrived and all the parents were beginning to fill the stands as well the other team was full into their warm-ups.

The referees blew the whistle and the game was about to begin. I looked at the coaches and said.

"God damn, it's a beautiful day for football."

The coaches smiled and agreed and could see that I was pumped again woo hoo!

We won the coin toss again and we asked to receive. I wanted to smash face right away now this team we were playing thought they knew our team from the last thrashing they gave us so I used this in the huddle to pump up the kids. As we took to the field we huddled up and I told the kids this team is expecting one thing and we are going to teach them another, let's pump it up and lets introduce them to smash face.

Justin called the play as the kids lined up, I stood back and watched the pile move as the kids ran the play and moved the ball well. The kids picked up a first down on their first play. We got in the huddle again and I said to the kids.

"See kids, they don't know what to expect so lets score quick before they have time to adjust."

"Justin call the play". The kids lined up and I watched as the pile moved again, but this time the pile instead of falling was held up by the amount of kids pushing each way, it was like a blooper. The pile was so big no one could see Justin the ball carrier and the pile kind of stood stagnated for what seemed an eternity with arms and legs pushing and pulling. Then all of a sudden Justin popped out of the other side of the pile on his feet with the ball and his head down still pushing with his arms.

I could hear the coaches from the sidelines yelling.

"Run, Justin."

It was so comical, Justin took a second to look around and got his bearings, the only kid Justin could see was Kyle, his lead blocker who lead him through the pile. Kyle was gesturing to Justin to run and run Justin finally did with Kyle as an escort for about 40 yards for the touchdown. It was hilarious and as Kyle and Justin got in the end zone the bulk of the kids on both teams were still struggling in the pile I kid you not, it was to funny.

The Warriors lead 6-0. Justin and Kyle were celebrating in the end zone as the rest of the kids began to realize what had happened. I thought, I have to see if John the cameraman got this on tape, as it would make a great blooper. We all ran down to the end of the field to set up for our infamous point after. Danny lined up the snap came and big Dan put the ball through the uprights perfectly and the crowd exploded, as did the kids. It was our first point after Dan ran over to me and gave me a hug he was so proud of himself I smiled and said.

"Atta boy Danny I knew you could do it son."

Damy's first feild
goal

Well it was great, here we were on their home field and just into the game and we had an 8-0 lead and our first point after. We kicked the ball to this team and they began as we cheered on our defense. The other team moved the ball okay but our defense stood tall as they approached our end zone and the defense forced the other team into a third and long and a punting situation. I thought on the sidelines great the defense held we get to run the ball some more and hopefully bury this team before they can get into the game.

The team set up for the punt and nobody saw it coming. It was a fake, instead of kicking the ball they ran it and caught us sleeping and scored from about 30 yards out. It was bad, but my compliments to the coaches on the other team it was a smart call. The other team attempted their point after and failed and the Warriors still lead 8-6 our sidelines went quiet as we awaited the kick. I headed out on the field with the kids and we huddled up. I told the kids don't worry about what happened, you're doing well here and the game is young lets pump it up and move this pile again. Justin called the play, I stood back and watched as the other team now adjusted to the offense and things bogged down.

Neither team could move the ball and the half time came with the two teams struggling on offense. The score remained 8-6 for the Warriors at half time. Dave took the kids into the end zone for his half time speech as I conferred with the coaches.

I told the coaches that things on the field were good but slow and that we had to have patience. I realized that Dave was right I was going to have to ignore the coach and his play selections. I told the coach to wait for the right time, the coach agreed but was persistent about this one kid, and the one play tailored for this kid. Anyway the second half began and the kids were ready, Dave had them all pumped up again. We began the second half and the defense shut down the team right away. We received the ball and as I went out on the field the coach was calling to me and asking me if I wanted this kid on the field. This meant this kid and the new play. I waved to the coach and yelled back.

"Yea, yea, in a minute."

We got in the huddle and I looked at the kids and said.

"We have the lead, the defense is playing well and it's the second half. Let's move the ball and get a drive going and get some first downs and take control of this game."

I looked at Justin and said.

"Come on kids, lets do it, call the play."

I stood back and watched as the kids ran the play. We were deep in our end and I thought let's play field position now.

The kids began to move the ball slowly but surely we picked up a first down. In the huddle I told the kids they were doing well and the rhythm was beginning to come. The kids ran the play and they picked up good yards. Every play now the coach was yelling out to me on the field.

"Sean, Do you want this kid on now?"

I kept waving him off as I felt the kids were creating a rhythm moving the ball now and we were getting out of our end. The kids continued to run the plays, we were moving and now the coach was getting crazy with the calling. I could not take it anymore so I motioned to send the kid in and send in the play. I knew in my heart it was wrong and we were going to get in to trouble but it was still his team and he was the Head Coach.

In the huddle, I told the kids the play and I could feel the animosity and concern from the kids. I told them to block hard and allow Justin the time to throw the ball. We broke and I stood back and watched and it happened the kids ran the play. Justin threw the ball and the other team intercepted the ball and ran it back to our 10 yard line. I couldn't stomach it I knew nothing good was going to come of that play. There it was the practice mentality of the coach as the game meant nothing to him. The coach forgot what the game meant to the kids, these kids took this serious now and as well they should. They were embarrassed enough at the start of this season.

I stood in the middle of the field and watched as the kids were visibly upset over the play and the results of the play. I could not believe I had allowed it to happen. Through no fault of the kids, the fault was mine for listening and allowing this to happen. I walked off the field and I was angry. I thought we had this team and all we had to do was be patient. I was so sick of saying this to people and as well, I was becoming sick of trying to prove ourselves.

I walked over to the sidelines as the defense took to the field, I could not even look at Jess. I was so ashamed of myself. Dave looked at me, smiled and shrugged his shoulders. The coach looked and said.

"If it had worked, we would have been heroes."

I walked by him and thought my God man it's not about you and me it's about the kids and their pride. I did not say anything I thought to myself Sean just get over it and keep quiet.

The other team scored a touchdown and took the lead 12-8. There was still plenty of time in the game and I had to re-focus. I went out onto the field with the kids and again I apologized in the huddle for calling the play. The kids smiled and told me not to worry about it. I told Justin to run the play and the kids did they ran the ball very well the rest of the game. We had about 3 good opportunities to score and take the lead back but we did not. I take most of the blame as I was out of the game mentally.

Now it's tough to describe how on the field you are so wrapped up with the kids, the game and the rhythm. However, I quickly found out how quick you can fall out of the rhythm. I was so far away from the kids and the zone. I think the kids knew but they still played well. I felt like a third leg on the field with the kids. The other team went on to score again late in the game and took the lead 18-8 and we just never got back into it. I felt so sorry for the kids. The game ended that way 18-8 and when the game ended I gathered up Jess and Kurt right away and headed out. I was still angry and did not want to say anything stupid and I felt it was better that I left.

The coach gathered the kids for the speech, I walked on past and got to the van, and we headed home. In the van I looked at Jess and said.

"That was my fault son not you kids, you kids played well and by all rights should have won that game even after the mistake. You kids took it to that team today and I think the other team and the coaches knew this. We just didn't score when we could of and I allowed outside interference at the crucial time of the game and that's my fault."

We got home and Kim brought the tape home and I was still upset and maybe I was wrong to get angry but what happened was stupid and should not have happened. Kim told me to take it easy and not get so worked up over it and she was right, it was done and over. The kids and I began to watch the tape. It was a good team, but I will always believe that if the game plan had been followed, we would of have smoked that team no doubt in my mind.

The kids went about their weekend. I then turned the tape off and vowed that this interference was never going to happen again. But if it did, I was going to leave the field and tell the coach that if he wanted to run a play he could go out on the field and do it himself.

This journey was between the kids, my son and me and I was not going to allow it anymore. The kids knew what to do, I knew what to do and so did Dave and we were doing fine up to now. I decided that I was going to apologize to the kids on practice Monday night and make this vow to the kids for the playoffs and recommit to the kids for the playoff run. I awaited Monday's practice and to see the kids as I left in an awful hurry after the game. I would like to reiterate here that nobody knew about the promise I made to my son Jess. This was between Jess and I and I think this is partly what angered me the most.

I did believe we could make this journey happen but I did not allow for outside influences and I felt that the bond between Jess and I was being threatened. I cherished the idea of being able to help my son and his teammates. I was delighted when the kids were doing well.

I admired how Jess never once mentioned the promise, to me or to anyone else. I decided from here on in I was going to make good on that promise no matter what or who stood in the way. I thought that maybe I would tell Kim and the coaches about this commitment and maybe they would understand my intensity and passion, but I decided this was between Jess and I and we were going to make it happen. It is hard to explain how I felt about this journey and the kids. All I knew was I gave my word to my son and I felt I had to honour this promise with Jess.

"End of Regular Season"

Record 2 wins 4 losses, we fell to the bottom of the "B" round.

Yahoo! The Playoffs:

The playoffs began approximately 2nd or 3rd week in October. Brrrr! The cold and snow would be slowly creeping in on these poor devils.

Four, teams per round being:
4 top teams "A" round
4 middles teams "B" round
4 bottom teams "C" round

Each round was a 3 game round robin affair and the 2 best records of the 4 teams made the final game of each round. Simple enough, right? So goes the format called the City finals and we were in and ready to rock.

Chapter 6

The Playoffs and The Drive

he boys and I went to practice Monday night and the boys ran off to play with the other players as I approached the coaches. I handed the coaches the tape and did not really have much to say to the coaches.

I think the Head coach knew that I was still upset over the play and game from the weekend past. We talked about the game and the play and I did appreciate the coach talking with me about the play. We put the play and the game behind us this night by mutual and unsaid consent.

We now had the playoffs coming and it was time to focus in, as these kids would need solid leadership in the playoffs. Dave showed up and we all began to talk about the kids and our concerns we had about the defense of our team. Dave and I expressed our concerns about a position on the defense that was having a tough time. We had expressed this concern earlier to the head coach and he understood what we were concerned about and agreed. He assured us that he would handle it this week.

It was time to change this spot as the team we played last weekend really exposed this weakness against us for two touchdowns.

Without trying to hurt anyone's feelings which was imperative to us. I think the head coach realized that the defense would have to be changed heading into the playoffs After the kids had their warm ups and the coaches finished their speech. I called the kids into the huddle with me, I looked at the kids and said.

"I apologize for Saturday's game, and more importantly I apologized for losing focus and the zone."

I explained that it was a tough thing to stay focused and live in the zone for a long period of time. I also told the kids how impressed I was with the way they kept focus and stayed in the game until the finish. I further told the kids that I was back and I was here to stay no matter what. I continued that we have the playoffs now and we need to really focus, as the other teams will really come after us now. I looked at the kids and assured them that if they would forgive me and put their faith in me again, we would rule the playoffs and I said.

"No one else, just us kids will rule and decide from here on in what this team will do and we will do what it takes." I asked the kids.

"What do you think?" The kids were so sweet they said.

"Don't worry about what happened last Saturday let's smash face and get ready." I smiled and said.

"Justin call the play." and the kids lined up.

I stood back and watched as the kids practiced the plays and thought how fortunate I was to be part of these kids and this team. These kids were truly special and a pleasure to be involved with. Practice went on this week fairly well.

The parents were still hopeful I felt of their little Warriors and so were the kids and the coaches. This little park we called home was now showing the signs of the season as the fall rolled in and with it the dampness and cold. The daylight was now quickly disappearing on us and fall was in the air. But the most exciting feeling was the atmosphere of the Warriors being in the B round of the playoffs.

In the middle of one of the practices this week the Head coach walked right in the middle of the practice scrimmage with the defense. We all stopped and watched as the coach made the change on defense that we had been asking for.

The Head coach changed the players around and stated that this change was a Head coach decision, the coach then walked away and Dave and I felt that he handled this as best as he could without hurting anyone. Dave and I felt this change was the final little adjustment now to create a dominating team.

As a blessing, the kid we changed from defense Dave I took on offense with us and this kid became a real asset to the offense of this team. All it takes sometimes is a slight change to discover a whole new set of talent with these kids. Practiced continued on and we were feeling pretty good about ourselves and confidence was high.

The Head coach continued to stress his new plays for the offense.

The kids headed into the playoffs as I would describe as the underdog. Once again the kids were at a disadvantage. The two top teams in the round of 4 teams were our first opponents. We had to travel out east of the city to the field of one of the top seed teams to start and our second game was against the other top seed team on their field tough start eh?

Our final game was against the weakest team statistically in the round, so I thought we have to prove ourselves right away in these playoffs and I don't think I would have wanted it any other way.

I thought once we knock off the two top teams the final game will be for fun and a little break awaiting the final and championship game. The thought of these kids even making the B round would have been a joke about 4 weeks ago.

Along with being underdogs in the numbers our poor little Warriors were on the road for all our games. We would not have another home game for the rest of the playoffs. Anyway, we were on the road and that is the way it had to be. Our first team was a strong solid team and I think were waiting for us for their first win in the playoff round. We practiced the kids and prepared the kids as much as we could knowing full well that the teams we met were now going to take every game very serious now.

I recall this week in practice, I think it was Thursday night the kids and I were down at the other end of the field awaiting the other coaches to set up their kids for practice. As we were in the huddle one of the kids noticed these two teenage kids in a pickup truck at the end of the field making out.

The teenagers were kissing up a storm and rolling around in the back of the truck, well when all the kids noticed this the kids began to call out to the teens. They were yelling out provocative suggestions to the teens. I looked at the kids and at first thought hey their boys and young boys at that, I kind of chuckled. I looked at Katherine who was standing there obviously embarrassed as the boys made their cat calls. Katherine was by far one of the true sparkplugs of this offense and above all else a true little lady. It hurt me as Kath looked like a fish out of water while the boys screamed and jeered.

I looked at the boys and snapped at the kids.

"HEY YOU BOYS HAVE A LADY present here, have a bit of respect boys."

The kids looked at me and went quiet. I laughed as, I think it was Bosco, who first went up to Katherine and began to apologize for his behavior to her. After Bosco the rest of the boys began to apologize to Kath, it was a great moment and a team moment and the boys showed some class I was proud of them.

All week in practice the coaches expressed greater concern over this team in the east we were facing, at this point now I wasn't listening to anymore skepticism anymore. I was going out to do a job now and so were these kids. Practice ended and all that was left now was the kids first playoff game. The coach called the kids in for his speech. We gathered around, the coach told them they were ready for the game and began to share his experience with them as he had been here before.

After the coach finished he allowed the other coaches to speak and they did. I had my turn to speak, instead of speaking I decided to yell and stir it up. I began by screaming, chanting and creating the frenzy again. After this the coach dismissed the kids for the evening and as they left the coaches would gather for the final game day preparations. Dave and I could sense the concern in the voices of the coach over the team we were to meet tomorrow. Pre game jitters and all, the Head coach was obviously concerned with this team we were facing tomorrow. I looked at the coach and said.

"Listen buddy, it's a done deal now these kids are going to win and win big and you can take that to the bank."

The coach looked and reluctantly agreed!

Dave reassured the coach telling him let the kids do what they do well and don't worry about it because it's really all up to these kids now. I think Dave was talking from experience. Dave was right we could do all we wanted but in the playoffs it was all going to come down to these kids and their heart and will on the field. I then further told the coach to stop worrying as these kids were going to win the B cup and that was all there was to it. I told the coaches get ready and hold on for the ride. After this we broke up and I grabbed the boys and headed home to get ready for battle tomorrow. On the way home I asked Jess if he was ready. Jess just smiled and said.

"Oh Yea Dad." I told Jess.

"It's time for the Warriors to go to war and I expect all the Warriors to be ready tomorrow."

I got the boys set up on the couches and told Kurt and Jess to try and get some sleep as I would need the both of them to be completely focused tomorrow. The boys agreed, I then turned to Kim and gave her this crazy little smile. I was teaching the kids it was the smile of a mad man, I said.

"I'm ready and I'm pumped and ready for battle." and then growled at her.

Kim just gave me that smile that I was becoming used to know, the smile that told me she understood the craziness but please Sean take it out on the kids not me. I have to say here that Kim was a good sport about all the madness and screaming. But as I smiled at her I thought, it's the same as I told the coaches batten down the hatches because now the ride really begins.

I then retired for the evening to store up some energy. I almost forgot to mention the other little gimmick I added to the kids ritual for their motivation. When Jess and I were headed to the field tonight for practice I just began to hum and sing to Jess. I guess I was getting pumped. Anyway out of the singing I developed this little fight song for the kids. I sang it to Jess and asked him what he thought.

He loved the song and said lets teach the team I agreed. When we got to the field that night, I called the kids into a huddle after the coaches sent the kids to do their laps. The kids came over to the coaches and me and the parents wondered what I was doing with them. As the kids gathered around, I explained the song and the reason for the song. The song was to let everyone know who you were and what it was you did.

I chose Bosco to be the lead singer because Bosco was feeling a bit left out of the team I felt. I thought this might help him feel good about himself. As the coaches called to me to ask what was going on, the kids and I quickly practiced the song and I told them we were going to surprise everyone. The kids were ready to go, so I told Bosco,

"Go ahead son, lead it off."

By now all the parents and coaches were standing around waiting to see what the kids were up to. Bosco began to run and the rest followed him and as they ran in a pack behind Bosco he began,

"WE'RE THE WARRIORS DON'T YOU KNOW."

The rest of the kids would repeat this as Bosco finished. Bosco then responded.

"GET OUT OF OUR WAY OR DOWN YOU'LL GO, WE ARE."

All the kids would join.

"WARRIORS, again Bosco. "WE ARE". the kids. "WARRIORS." and so on.

It was just like the fight songs you would hear the military would sing in the movies. As they ran in formation. I told the kids to continue repeating this as they ran their laps. I wandered over to the coaches and the parents, smiled, and said.

"Now the kids have their fight song and now the team is complete."

Some of the parents smiled and the coaches just gave me that look of okay Sean whatever you think. I was beginning to get this look a lot now and I enjoyed it, this expression usually told me that the kids and I were doing the right thing if you know what I mean.

Well that was it, the kids loved their fight song and they sung it well and looked good doing it. Also I believed it created and strengthened the camaraderie of these tiny Warriors. I felt it was the final piece in the mental preparation for these kids. I was going to send them in front of the other teams benches before the games chanting this song. We wanted to let the other team know that we were ready for battle.

Bzzzzzzzzzz YAHOOOOO, it came 6:00A.M. and up the stairs, I flew out of bed. I was wired again and wild, go figure eh! There was no time for the beauty of the morning or time for serenity it was the playoffs and there was time only for football. I began screaming as I came up the stairs.

"WAKE UP BOYS, IT'S TIME FOR SOME FOOTBALL." The boys got up and I began.

"GET IT UP, GET IT GOING, FOR TODAY WE DO BATTLE Ha Ha Ha."

Jess got into it right away. I would pump up Kurt and Kurt actually was getting on board now with the madness. I was glad for Kurt, as it was a great time and he should enjoy it with us. The boys ate and put on their equipment as they prepared for battle.

I now took a moment to look out the window and saw that it was a great morning. It was sunny, bright a beautiful fall morning. I turned to the boys and growled out loud and screamed,

"It's a great day for some football kids."

Dave and his son were headed over to the house and we were going to pick up Kyle and head out together this morning. The boys and I headed outside and we began tossing the ball around and Dave pulled up with his son Gregory. As Gregory stepped out of the car, I yelled at him.

"Are you ready?"

I think I scared the hell out of the kid. Greg looked at me and said.

"Yes coach." but more importantly Dave replied.

"Yea I'm ready."

I thought, great Dave is into it and ready. We picked up Kyle and headed out to the field, we painted up Kyle and Greg's faces as we drove out. It was a real adventure way out to the boon docks Dave and I kept telling the kids were going to Bengal land to kick butt. We began to chant with the kids.

"WHAT DO WE WANT FOR BREAKFAST?" and the kids would reply.

"BENGALS, BENGALS" it was a blast.

Dave and I managed to find the field and for the first time we were a bit late. To my pleasure as we pulled up the Warriors were all there and waiting. I pulled up and looked at my kids all huddled around on the field just mingling and the parents doing the same. I stopped the van, looked at Dave and said.

"Are you ready, bud?"

Dave nodded and we jumped out of the van and I screamed like I never screamed before.

"WARRIORS" with my hands up in the air. The kids that were mingling began screaming back at me.

"WARRIORS."

We all realized it was time to start the frenzy and madness. I'm sure the whole world heard us and that was great, I wanted the world to know we were here. Dave and I walked up to the kids and began screaming.

I was happy we were ready and now the field was beginning to wake up. Dave began to warm the kids up and I just had a compelling feeling to go and stir it up a bit more. I wasn't sure what but I had to do some thing. I headed over to our parents as I got to them I bellowed at them as they stood around." Are you ready for some football people". The parents looked at me and replied we're ready.

I thought I got them up, now it was time to wander down to the other team and introduce myself to these people. I recall as I was walking over to the canteen where the other team and their parents were gathered one of the parents came up to me and said.

"Hey Coach, are you all right?" I turned to the parent and said.

"I'm great and I'm ready for some football" and smiled, the parent chuckled at me.

I then proceeded over to the table and the coffee, I walked up and there were all these parents serving coffee and donuts and socializing. I walked up to the table and I yelled Good morning to the poor woman serving the coffee, the woman almost jumped out of her skin. I asked for a coffee and as she served me, I yelled again.

"It's a great day for some football, isn't it?"

The parents around me were looking and wondering what all the screaming was about and I did feel sorry for the woman serving. I didn't mean to be so obnoxious but I was so pumped and I had to let it out. I headed back to our sidelines and thought that was enough energy for now, they now knew we were here.

I recall as I walked back over Dave and the kids were looking at me and Dave shook his head with a smile. Dave knew what I was up too.

Dave and I ran the kids through some practice plays as we prepared, all the time screaming with the kids and pumping them up at every chance. The coaches arrived and I think some of our parents might have went to the coaches and told them how wired we were. I never found out if they did or not and who cares it was playoff football now.

The game was about to begin and Dave and I got all the kids in a huddle and told the kids to remember what happened last week, the loss!

We told the kids to think about that game, as they thought I said remember the bad taste in your mouth after you lost I asked the kids.

"Did you enjoy losing?" The kids all screamed.

"No Coach" I then said.

"Today boys and girls we give all we have and we walk off this field as victors today, no more bad taste right?" The kids replied.

"Let's Smash Face coach." I laughed and said.

"Kids are you with me?" They all replied.

"Yes." I screamed.

"Lets Smash face."

All the kids began screaming and hitting each other's pads and heading to the zone. We won the toss and asked to have the ball first. The game began and we received the ball from the other teams kick off and I headed out to the field with the kids. We got in the huddle and I looked at the kids and their painted little faces and said.

"We have the ball, we have the zone, let's go smash face pump it up kids. Justin call the play."

I stood back and the kids lined up and Justin in his confident manner barked out the call. He was great to watch Justin had taken full control of this team and as I thought, his leadership qualities were coming through like gang-busters. It was marvelous to watch he was a true leader. The kids ran the play and it took about 5 plays of smash face and the kids were running the ball through the end zone dancing and celebrating as they scored their first touch down of this playoff to take the lead early 6-0 Warriors. We were all jumping around, hugging each other and chanting Warriors. It was fantastic, the kids were smoking and smoking early. Just what we needed being the under dog and being in strange surroundings. We attempted our point after and yes you guessed it we were unsuccessful but it did not matter the kids were tripping now. We kicked the ball back as the celebrating calmed down and we watched as the defense took the field to hold.

I do not think the coaches on the other team could believe how excited the kids and I would get on the field together when the kids did well. The defense dug their feet in and the other team began their offense as we cheered.

It took two plays the now complete defense we talked about shut down the other teams offense and they had to kick to us again. I remember thinking great, it will be a complete team effort here again today.

As the ball came down in front of me from the other teams punt, our return man fumbled the ball and the other team recovered the ball on about our 20-yard line. I couldn't believe it. I thought to myself this was tough after stopping the team, we give the ball right back. We had to be strong and hold this team. We began to cheer on the defense again and the defense did play it tough but the other team banged the ball in after their third play and tied the game up with us. I felt so bad for the defense, but we had to stay in it, we had to keep focus. The other team kicked their point after and took the lead 8-6 agghhh.

We decided to slow it down a bit on offense and play ball control offense, well this style of ball went on for the rest of the first half. The two teams struggled to gain yards but we were gaining field position on the team when the ref blew the whistle to call half time. It was Bengals 8 Warriors 6.

It actually was a great half, minus our mistake. Dave took the kids into the end zone for his half time speech and I conferred with the coaches on the sidelines. I told the coaches I was rather concerned with the lack of yards our kids were picking up on our plays. I also complimented the other coach on the defensive play of our kids. I told the head coach that the coach of the other team was physically taking his kids and lining the kids up in front of where we were lining up to run and I felt that the refs shouldn't allow this. The other team was constantly jumping off side and not being called for it. I said its not right, our kids practice hard to be disciplined on the field and its not fair for our kids to watch these other kids get away with this.

The head coach agreed and we then decided we were going to open the offense up a bit but only the plays our kids knew and this meant running the ball outside with lead blockers instead of up the gut. We decided to see if the other coach on the field could respond quickly enough to running outside instead of inside.

I told the coach.

"It's time to open these kids up a bit." The coach agreed. I also said.

"I am not blaming anyone but we can't make mistakes and expect to win." He agreed again.

The game had slowed right down after the first two quick scores but the game was intense, you could feel the intensity on both sides of the field. I witnessed a bit of taunting and teasing going on between the kids on the field. However, it was the playoffs and my compliments to the other kids and their coaches.

Dave returned with the kids, all freshly pumped up, again thanks Dave for your great work with the kids at the half time breaks. I had quietly been practicing our kids on offense with Dave on some simple changes to our lead blocking to try to change things up to fool the other team. I consulted with Dave quickly as the second half was beginning and we agreed it was time to try it.

I also told Dave that I had noticed two of the kids on the other team's defense looked weak in their size and stature. One of the kids was playing outside and he was very small compared to our lead blocker. I thought, if we ran at this kid we could run him over and for once we had size advantage over another team. Dave agreed. Also there was another kid on the line to the right of our formation, and he was rolling his hands up into his sleeves to keep warm and it was not really that cold of a morning. It actually was somewhat mild. I told Dave that we would change our formation and bull this kid over as well. Dave agreed and we headed into the second half with the game plan.

The second half began and we kicked the ball to the other team to start. The other team lined up and the parents of both teams now were cheering on their kids, as well the cheerleaders both theirs and ours were in full motion and cheering on their respective teams. The atmosphere was now one of intensity, it was great.

Our defense shutdown the other teams offense right away and I felt good as it seemed that the defense was now ready to control this other team. From the sidelines we were all cheering on the defense as it worked its magic. With the ball being turned over, I headed out to the field with the kids and we congratulated the kids on defense as we passed each other. I could feel the energy coming.

In the huddle, we started the chanting, "WHO ARE WE."

I began to explain the game plan for the second half to the kids. I told the kids the changes we were going to make and made sure all the kids were comfortable with the plan. They all agreed with the changes and were confident with the plays, as we had practiced them. After mutual agreement, I looked at Kyle and Danny, our lead blockers and told them to start screaming and growling out there. Let's get into this kids and start some smash face here.

I told Justin to call the play and as he did I could hear them all screaming and growling at the other team as they lined up for the play.

I remember both the refs and the other coaches on the field looking at the kids and me as if we were crazy. Well the smash face took over and the power came to the kids. The changes worked great and the kids pounded the ball into the end zone with relative ease and took a 12-8 lead over this top seed team in the middle of the third quarter. The kids were started to really come together and it was rewarding to watch.

On the sidelines, both our team and the parents were all celebrating the score and it was fun. We had to kick the ball back to this team as well we had to try our point after again. Well we missed again and I could see the parents on the sidelines were having a great time with this part of the game. It was rather comical, the kids would try hard but they just could not get it and it was now becoming like a burden to the kids. I think the kids now wanted to run the ball on points after instead of kicking. They knew they could run the ball when they wanted to but the kick was the head coaches call and we had to try. I was of the belief that it didn't matter we would score enough majors on the ground now that we didn't have to worry about points after for a kick.

I tried to tell the kids this but they were so determined now to be good that they did not want to fail at anything.

After all this we kicked the ball back to the other team with the lead in hand and the third quarter almost over now. I think it took two plays and this other team made their mistake and our defense swarmed and recovered the ball after the other team fumbled the ball on about their 30-yard line. Our kids and parents went wild with celebration, our defense now had taken over the game and our offense was poised to jump in and put the final nail in the coffin of this our first playoff game. The other teams sidelines and parents were visibly upset over the Warriors and their domination now of the field.

The kids and I took to the field and in the huddle after congratulating our defense we all looked at each other and starting chanting end zone, end zone, as the refs set up after the turnover. I got the kids to focus in and I told the kids.

It was slow at first but that was good we had the lead and the game was winding down and I thought a bit of ball control would be good right now.

I told Justin to start running the ball right side at the small kid on the other team's defense that I had mentioned earlier. It worked like a charm, as the little Warriors pounded the ball into the end zone for their second major of the half. The kids and the sidelines were celebrating while these little troopers were taking a commanding lead. The lead now was 18-8 for the Warriors and it was exhilarating. The parents and kids were all clapping and cheering. These little kids that were to small, young and inexperienced to win. Now they had one of the top ranked teams by the throat and poised to defeat this team on their home field.

After all the celebrating we kicked the ball back to this team and once again this team failed to move the ball on offense as our defense took the ball away and gave it back to our offense. The game was now coming to a close and it was obvious who the better team was. Our Warriors were flying high and swarming on the field now like a pack of wild dogs the energy level was amazing. The game was almost over now and I could see that the parents and the coaches were pleased with the kid's performance. Most importantly, the kids were pleased with themselves.

The other team tried to mount a come back but the defense just totally annihilated the other team to a point that the other team could not move. It was like our defense had become a huge blanket and smothered the other team into submission.

The game ended and the Warriors won 18-8 and the celebration began. The Warriors had a leg up in the playoffs, one game one win as the parents and kids gathered after shaking hands with the other team. I chuckled to myself just like I thought, one team down and one to go. We will knock off the top teams in this round. I noticed the other team and their coaches did not take this loss well. I don't blame them it's their field and we were the underdog. I would be upset too but for these little misfits, it was a sign of things to come. These kids now were homed in and convinced that they could do whatever they wanted to do, as long as they believed in themselves and played as a team. I remember the head coach called all the kids and parents into a huddle amongst all the hysteria going on. As the coach began to get things calmed down he invited all the kids and parents to a local restaurant that he knew to celebrate the victory.

I thought this is good since this journey had begun, the kids, the parents and the coaches had really never sat down and celebrated and socialized other than at the practice field and the games. I thought this was a good idea we might as well all bond now. All we had to do was follow the kids lead and as they had shown the bonding would be natural as we were all now were beginning to feel a part of this journey that our kids were taking us on.

After the coach made a little speech and his invite to the kids we all set out to this local restaurant for our first real victory celebration. I got in the van with Dave and the kids and we were still all pumped up, we were chanting and going over every play of the game together. We got to the restaurant and we all piled out of the van. As we headed into this place, I looked at the kids from behind and thought oh my God we are about to unleash this tribe on this poor restaurant. Heaven help the owner and if the owner was the coaches friend I thought that might change after these kids get through here.

All still in their football gear and war paint still on, these kids descended on the restaurant and in their unique fashion took over the place.

I entered the building and the kids were running all over the place and creating havoc from one end to the other. I saw a few people at a table and the expressions on their faces said it all. They looked as though they were in shock as the herd of kids came streaming in and as usual, wild and still fired up. The owner corralled the kids in the back section of the restaurant and I must say the people and the manager were very good to the kids and the parents. The kids were served pizza and as they waited, the owner put the videotape of the game on the screen so the kids could watch their game as they ate and partied.

All I could hear was the cheering and chanting from the kids in the back as they watched the tape. The adults all kind of resigned to the bar of the restaurant and gathered around to sit and chat. As we were talking, I remember I got up and headed back to the kids. I walked in and the room was glorious, all of them in their uniforms and sitting together and having a great time. I stood in the middle of the room and thought well hell if they can make some noise so can I put my hands up and screamed.

"WARRIORS."

The kids went crazy the energy in the room was incredible, I could feel the energy from everyone. I began to walk around the tables and congratulated the kids one by one on their performance today and as I was doing this I heard this little voice from behind me call." Daddy".

I turned and looked and amongst all the yelling and confusion there was my little Jacob sitting at a table with the little cheerleaders of the team.

They looked so quaint and sweet, I walked over to Jake and said hello to the girls and bent over and told Jake that I loved him and gave him a kiss and a hug. I sometimes forgot that he was left out of the action and the excitement and it was special when he reminded me that he was still there. I talked to Jake and the girls for a bit and complimented the girls on their hard work. Then the pizza arrived and things became quiet as the kids dug into their food. This was my cue to go and talk with the coaches and Dave. I sat down at the bar with Dave and the parents who were all settled now in their booths and having a good time chatting it up with each other. I looked at Dave and said.

"This is good." I then laughed and said.

"Dave that team wasn't as good as we heard." Dave just laughed.

It was then that the coach sat down beside me and Dave got up to go to the bathroom. I looked at the coach and said.

"We're on our way."

I said the kids were perfect other than one play and they played a good game and deserved the victory today. The coach agreed. The coach then looked at me and said.

"We haven't beaten that team in years Sean." I said.

"Your kidding me." The coach replied.

"We haven't won against them in years."

It was then I remembered last year that this was the team that knocked us out of the A round of the playoffs. I had forgotten this. God, that was a miserable day and a miserable game it was funny because I do not usually forget things like that. Anyway, I said to the coach with a smile.

"I guess that's over now."

The coach laughed and we began to talk about the game after a while the celebration began to break up and we all headed home with the kids and a 1-0 record in the playoffs.

When we got home we put the tape on again to watch, as I did not see much of it in the restaurant. Dave headed out and Jess and I sat down and watched the tape together. The boys and Kim went about their weekend.

1st victory over the Bengals
in 5 years pizza party

I think it was the next day that Jess and I were talking about the game and he told me that one of the kids on the other team told him that they would beat us in the B cup game. I asked Jess what he replied to the kid and he said that he just looked at the kid and said whatever. I congratulated Jess and he told me that the kid seemed angry. I told Jess that if the kid wanted to beat you they had their chance yesterday and they did not do a very good job of it. I then told Jess.

"You handled it well son, don't let anyone bother you like that you and your teammates do the talking where it counts and that's on the field". Just ignore that kind of stuff and if yesterday was any indication of that team's performance. That kid should worry about making the B cup let alone winning it, but I will tell you something." I know one team that will be in that championship for sure and that's the WARRIORS and we will take out whoever we have to." Jess smiled and nodded his head in agreement.

<u>Second Playoff. (Game Battle Royal)</u>

Practice Monday night I felt a sense of relief and excitement. I think a renewed excitement from the parents, kids and the coaches. For the coaches it must have been a pleasure to see their kids finally get that monkey off their backs from that team. That is a long time to be owned by another team. As the boys ran off to play I handed the tape to the coaches and made my comments and recommendations. I also complimented the coach on the final change on defense which was a definite asset to the whole team on Saturday, the coach agreed.

I began to get a sense that the coaches slowly believed in the kids now and I was happy with this. The kids just won 3 of their last 4 games after their horrendous start. The coaches began practice and we began to prepare the kids for what we were to find would be the most intense and exciting game of football I have ever been involved in.

We practiced the kids on the basics with emphasis on the kicking game. The kicking game was good other than the point after attempts but I wanted it perfected. I knew we would have to depend on this part of our game in the coming weeks.

I talked about the final change on defense the coach made well we made another slight adjustment on Saturday to the defense. While we were in the game in the second half I suggested to the head coach to put Kyle on the defensive line as Kyle was the biggest kid on our team. I told the coach that we have to use his size more. He was to go in on defense and cause havoc to the opposing teams offensive line. Well Kyle did a fantastic job on Saturday on defense, he was so big and overpowering he completely disrupted the other teams offense. Another diamond in the rough we had found and a gem he would turn out to be. I know it was demanding for the kid to play both ways but I knew Kyle personally and I knew he could handle it.

The coaches approved of this change and like me knew Kyle would only strengthen an already dominating defense. We practiced all week and it went pretty well other than the coach trying to add new plays to our offense. Again Dave and I struggled with this and reassured the kids that the only plays would be smash face and the kids hung in with Dave and I.

This week in practice I think it was Wednesday night, Katherine approached me and said.

"Hey coach, you know the team we face this weekend, one of the kids on the team is in my class at school." I looked and said.

"'Well that's good Kath." She continued to say.

"He came up to me today and said that his team wasn't sure about beating us this weekend." I smiled at Kath and said.

"I guess news about you kids is getting around this league and that's good. What do you think Kath, should they be worried about us?" Kath looked at me and growled at me and said.

"Yes they should." I then looked at Kath and said.

"Next time the little guy comes up to you and talks about the game and our team, just do what you just did to me." She looked confused and I said.

"Just growl at him with that face you make, okay sweetheart." Kath agreed and I never gave it another thought other than I guess the message these kids sent to this league four short weeks ago, has been received.

The team we were facing on Saturday had come to our field at the start of the season and pulverized our kids. I recall that they taunted and teased our kids, as I stood helpless on the sideline. This was I think the first game of the season, all I could think was it was time for our kids to go to their park and kick their butts. I would like to talk about how this lady Katherine and the other lady on our squad of Warriors woke me up and taught me about myself.

Katherine was beautiful, she was so intense focused and so physical if any one wandered into Kath's area on the field. Which we dubbed her home she'd lay a smack on the kid that would not be easily forgotten.

Kath played the corner and played it to perfection. I also took her on offense with me and as with Jess and the other kids, Kath would do whatever was asked of her no question and always gave 150 percent. She was a blessing to have as well as the other lady on the squad. These two girls changed what I believed for years.

I was one of those who believed that the football field was no place for a girl and boy, did these two girls open my eyes to my ignorance. Thanks to these girls, especially when it came to Kath. This little lady could easily play with the best and rule, thanks girls.

Back to Katherine's little story. She came back to me the very next night at practice and said.

"Hey coach." I turned and asked, "Yes Kath."

She began to tell me that this same boy approached her today again and asked about the game on Saturday. I asked.

"What did you tell him, Kath?"

She looked at me and growled at me with such intensity. I laughed and asked what the kid did and she told me he was scared and turned away from her. I smiled and said.

"Good girl Kath, go join practice."

As I had said, she would do whatever you asked her to do no questions asked. She was beautiful and I felt somewhat bad for the kid she scared, but it was playoff time. All week long the coaches again expressed great concern over facing the team on Saturday. Again, I tried to reassure the coaches and again told the coach not to worry, it's a done deal. These kids were going to win and take the B cup championship and you have to believe this beyond the shadow of a doubt. Anyway, that was all I was going to say. I knew what we had to do and so did the kids, and we were just going to do it. Friday night's practice came and with the final preparation the coaches called practice and brought the parents and kids in for the final game day speech. We all had our chance to speak to the kids as they huddled around us. Speak we did, we pumped the kids and again I sent them on their way to the zone before the coach dismissed them for the evening. Dave and I met in the tiny park as everyone left the park now in deep twilight by the end of our practice. The more I was around this little park the more I grew fond of it. It was not much but it was home for these kids. It was getting darker faster with fall in the air now, as we talked in the parking lot about tomorrow's game I admired the park and the kids. I remember hearing the concerns of the coaches as I wandered off into thought. I really did not want to listen, I thought what a change these kids have made, and how proud of them I was. We called it quits and Dave and I gathered the kids and headed home.

I looked at Jess in the van, smiled at him, and said.

"Son, tomorrow will be a tough game but we have to stick together and stand strong. All of you have to stand together tomorrow and I will stand with you and smash face will reign." Jess and I began to laugh.

Buzzzzzzzzzzz went the alarm and up pumped Dad to get the boys into the morning pre game rituals. I began the screaming, dancing and zoning. Dave and his son were on their way and I told the boys its time for the game. We headed outside to wait for Dave and Greg and as they arrived we headed to the field. In the van we would apply the war paint and pump the kids up. I told Dave that it seemed that our kids were showing up at the fields earlier every week and this I appreciated. It showed me the kids wanted to play now and wanted to be ready.

The morning again was another beautiful, bright fall morning. Other than the second game we were blessed with a real string of fine weather each Saturday morning and I loved it.

As we approached the field this morning that was hidden away behind a school in this neighborhood, I remember getting an uneasy feeling as we approached. I did not say anything. As we pulled into the yard I saw a silhouette of a player leaning against the fence post with the arms folded, resembling to me a gangster from the 60s. I thought that he must be the opposition's kid. We were early but I thought this was ridiculous. How early can a kid arrive at a game?

As we drew closer I began to recognize the figure in the sun, it was Katherine. I looked at Dave and said.

"This is scary, buddy." We pulled up and I rolled down the window, smiled, and said.

"Good morning Kath, how you doing?" Kath just looked at me and I could not believe the intensity in her eyes and her face she looked like she was ready to blow up. I told Kath to hop in and she said no, she would run along behind. As I drove off, I looked at Dave and he looked at me and we both laughed.

We pulled up in the parking lot and the first thought I had when I looked at the field was that it was barren and cold the field had no character, no feeling. It's hard to explain but it reminded me of this movie I had watched called the Wanderers and it took me back to the field in that movie where the big gang fight took place and how ugly the fight and the gangs were in the movie. The field was very intimidating and cold. I know this might sound crazy, but all the fields that we had visited had their own little character and reflection of the team based there. The feeling I got from this field was nothing short of eerie.

We all piled out and walked out on to the field the kids all began to show up now and Dave and I were getting the kids pumped up and painted.

I recall this one man came walking in when I was painting up one of our smaller kids. This man had a Viking jacket on, the team we were to face today, as the man approached and saw me applying the paint he made a gesture of disgust towards me. Now I always left the battling up to the kids but I think the eerie feelings and the tension I felt almost drove me to get up and ask if he had a problem. I decided against it. I finished painting the kid and headed down to our end of the field.

The coaches arrived as did the parents and the cheerleaders we were getting ready to start and I could not shake this uneasy feeling. It was so bad I felt you could smell it. I looked up at the sky and it was a sea of blue and the sun was bright and I thought, Sean don't let it bother you, it's a great day for football so start zoning in. The refs appeared as did the other team and their spectators and things were beginning to hum, the field now was showing signs of life. I looked over at this team as they practiced and they looked big and drag down tough and I knew this game was not going to be easy. Just before the game was to start I walked over to Kim. Who was with the other mothers and the cheerleaders to say hello and get a kiss for luck. As I approached Kim I could see she was visibly upset about something.

Now you have to know Kim and I do not recall ever seeing her this upset before. I walked up and asked what was wrong. Kim began to rant and rave about how ignorant the people running the game had been to our parents and especially our cameraman John. Apparently the woman in charge refused to let John set up the video and was very ignorant in telling him so. Then she went on about the other parents being rude and cold towards the kids and our parents. I looked at Kim and told her not to worry about it. As I turned to walk back to our team, Kim called me and said.

"Sean, beat this team."

Wow I looked at Kim and I thought Kim would never talk like that no matter whose kids they were. Kim just was not like this I smiled and winked at her and headed to our bench. As I walked I looked at our team and I could see the intimidation in our coaches it was like everyone was walking on egg shells. I looked at the head coach and he began to walk towards me and that was it, I kind of lost it. I stormed over to the table where all these people from the other team were set up with trophies and a game ball on a mount of a trophy awaiting the game. I was ticked now and the head coach knew it. I headed over to the table. When I got to there I raised my voice, and said,

"GOOD MORNING, A LOVELY DAY FOR FOOTBALL EH."

The woman at the table looked at me in contempt, I grabbed the ball off the stand they had it on, almost like a shrine and with disrespect I said.

"What's this?" The woman quietly said.

"The game ball." I laughed and said.

"So, what." I dropped the ball back on its stoop and said.

"Come on, let's play some football."

I turned and walked back to the bench and that was it, I was zoned, I was ready and I wanted to rumble. I looked at the coach and he was shaking his head laughing at me while I approached our bench. I got to the kids and I began screaming like a wild man, the coach knew what was going on, the kids started screaming and the frenzy began and so did the game.

We received first and I went out on the field with the kids as we took the field and we ran by the other teams table and bench and I was screaming like a nut and so were the kids. I thought to myself your not going to intimidate us we are too good for that now.

I got in the huddle with the kids and reminded them that these kids thought we were the same team they defeated way back at the start of the season. I told the kids.

"Let's introduce them to the new Warriors and smash face." I yelled in the huddle.

"Pump it up kids, Justin call the play."

I stood back and the kids took over. It couldn't of worked any better 1,2, and 3 plays and Justin was doing his little patented dance in the end zone for a 6-0 Warrior lead. Our kids just mowed down their defense, it was almost embarrassing to watch. The field was excited as the kids and I celebrated and the parents cheered us on. I recall I looked at the other teams bench and smiled at the coaches and thought to myself this will be a war today and were declaring it on you.

After things calmed down somewhat, we attempted our point after and you know what happened, the Warriors lead 6-0. Anyway, we kicked the ball back to the other team and it happened on the kick return, the other team blew through our return team and scored the major. In about 10 seconds and it was 6-6. The other team failed on their point after attempt and it stayed tied for the moment.

On the return of the punt there was a blatant clip block thrown on Katherine that freed the kid on the other team to score and the ref was right at the clip and didn't call it. Our parents were right there and the parents began getting on the refs case and I don't blame them. I later found out that we all believed this ref was intimidated as well as everyone else. I looked at the Head coach and said you have to say something or else some one is going to get hurt here and its not fair to the kids. The coach agreed and began to badger the ref. We didn't mean to bother the ref but when he's right there at the play he has to call it. That's what he's paid to do.

The team kicked the ball back to us and we set up about mid field. Our kids came out on the field ready again, I pumped the kids up in the huddle and told Justin to call the play and the kids moved the ball again as I stood back and watched them. The other team was hitting and hitting hard. I will give the other team this, their kids knew how to hit. I worried about our smaller kids getting hurt but I thought it's the game and we had to be just as intense. There also was some taunting going on between the kids and believe me, the tension was so bad you could cut it with a knife.

The kids pounded the ball in again with relative ease and I was so proud of the way they were not backing down from this bruising team, even our little ones stood in there. The Warriors took the lead and we began to run for our points after and got the point, go figure eh, the Warriors had the lead near the end of the first quarter. We kicked the ball back to the team and yes it happened again, same side, same play, same block from behind the other team scored again. Our parents were getting very upset with the refs now, both plays happened right in front of them.

I looked at the coach on the sidelines and said.

"We can't keep up with this and you know it, we can't allow them to score so quickly after we do."

All the time the parents of the other team as well the team, were celebrating and the other team were successful on their kick after and tied it up. The coach began to talk to the unit of kids that were allowing these touchdowns and Dave was trying to get them pumped up and refocused. It hurt to allow two majors in two plays. The other team kicked the ball back to us and I took to the field again with the kids. In the huddle, I asked the kids how they were doing with all the bullshit and hitting going on. These little beauties did not seem to let it bother them at all.

I rallied the kids and told Justin to call the play. I stood back and watched the hitting which was getting nasty and vicious both ways. I was surprised with some of our kids. The team held our offense and we had to kick the ball back and the second quarter was now winding down.

Well you guessed it, the third time was a charm, and with the charm came the third touchdown for the other team to take a 19-13 lead. We were all shocked, three kicks and three scores. I could not believe it and this time there was no clip or penalty missed by the refs I began to feel our sidelines beginning to get upset over the turn of events. Our kids began to get injuries now our sideline began to resemble an infirmary. The other team was celebrating as they failed at the single point and took the lead 19-13 with little time left in this wild first half. Dave was on the sidelines trying to rally the troops as well were the other coaches as we awaited the kick. I remember thinking to myself we have to tie it up before the half time break. I refused to go into the half time break trailing we received the ball and set up on about our 50-yard line.

I ran out on the field with the kids and the field was really buzzing now with the other team still excited over their lead. I got in the huddle and told the kids not to worry about the lead, just smash face here and tie this thing up. I looked into the faces of the kids and for the most the kids seemed to be holding up pretty well to this bizarre half of football. I told the kids to stay focused here, do what we do best and disregard all the confusion around us.

This is when I began to get on my knees with the kids in the huddle, and put my hand out. As I did this I told the kids to put their hands on mine and I began to shake and vibrate my hand. I would get quiet and I told the kids to feel the power and take the power from me and put it into your own hands. The kids would start shaking their hands and it was like a little séance was being held in the middle of the field but it seemed to work for the kids. We broke the huddle and I stood back as Justin barked out the play and the kids began to move the ball again.

They were so impressive to watch, again the other kids were bigger and this time a very physical team but our little Warriors were still pushing them out of their way.

As I watched from behind, I could see that the kids on both sides were giving everything they had and it was a fantastic struggle of the wills of both teams. It took about five plays and once again our kids were dancing in the end zone celebrating their touchdown, it was a beautiful drive. The first half was almost over and the kids punched it in for the tie, all we had to do was get a single point. The kids lined up, ran the play and we missed but we were tied. The kids were celebrating as well as their parents. It was turning into a roller coaster of emotions for all involved in this struggle.

We kicked the ball back with only about a minute to go in the first half and all I could think on the sidelines was come on kids hold this team and lets go into the half tied up. Well we finally began to shutdown the kick returns by this team, thanks to the kids on the field and thanks to the coaches getting our kids into the zone. The other team set up their offense and our defense shut them down and I had this sense of relief come over me on the sidelines. I thought, great the defense is getting pumped and aggressive now. The other team kicked to us and we set up on the field and began to run our offense.

I told the kids in the huddle lets just run the ball out and regroup for the second half, we ran two plays and the half ended. Just before the play ended

Justin got hit hard as he went down and Justin began to lose it and I don't blame him, the poor kid, he was taking a beating today. Justin turned to me and began giving me shit and exploding at me. I tried to calm him down as we walked off the field together and I could not. The kid was frustrated and tired of being hit. As we walked of the field the Head coach approached Justin and called him over to the sidelines. I walked up as Dave took all the other kids into the end zone. I looked at the coach and Justin and said.

"I understand Justin and if you don't want to continue we will let Danny carry the ball in the second half and you can sit and watch."

I did not mean to be insensitive to the kid but I knew the kid was tough and could take it. Justin was just frustrated and I thought by me saying this it would anger him to prove to me that he could take it. I also knew that this was Justin's team. I knew he would not allow anyone to run this offense unless he was on the sidelines on a stretcher. Even then, I think this kid would try to take the field when called to.

The coach took Justin off on their own to talk and I headed off to the end of the field alone to have a break. I knelt down, began to relax a bit and tried to notice the beautiful morning around us. As I sat the other coach came over and I said that I will talk later, right now I need a break and the coach left.

The game we were in was unbelievable. I knew one thing we were going to win this game and it was going to take everything these kids had. I headed back to our sidelines. I saw Justin and the coach and Justin seemed settled now. The coach and Justin came up to me and I looked at Justin and said.

"Well what is it, does Danny run this team or not?" Justin looked and said. "Coach, I'm coming back out with you." I smiled and said.

"I knew you would Justin, we have a job to do here, son."

I thanked the coach for talking to Justin and getting Justin pumped. I turned to look at Dave as he was returning with the troops all pumped and ready to go.

At this moment one of the fathers of the kids came up to me and was visibly upset. He began to tell me that he had just laid into the referees about the late hits, the clips, and the viciousness of this other team. As I had mentioned earlier, we had about 6 kids out with injury and one them was going to the hospital after the game to have his neck checked after a vicious face mask pull. This father went on to say that he had warned the ref that if another kid got hurt as a result of dirty play that he would take it up with the refs at the end of the game. He also told the ref that he had now been warned. At the conclusion of this talk to me the father looked at me and said.

"Now don't you worry anymore about it, just go out there with the kids and beat this team." I smiled and said.

"oh yea Thanks."

The father returned to the other side with the rest of the parents and I thought my God are the parents ever into this game. It was hard to see everything when you are on the field but I was told later, by many how wild this game was. Anyway, the coach looked at me next and said.

"Don't worry about Justin." I smiled and said.

"Great, let's get this thing started, we got a football game to win here." The coach smiled.

As we spoke the referees were setting up for the second half, we all began to get ready and we kicked the ball off to start the second half. Our defense took to the field and began to dominate this teams offense the defense forced the team to kick the ball to us. We set up the offense and got in the huddle, I looked and began pumping up the kids, again I stood back and watched as Justin and the kids struggled to pick up yards. We tried but had to kick, unlike the first half the second half turned into a defensive battle and a game of field position.

This I liked, we fought back and forth for most of the third quarter. I recall the Head coach yelling "Number 25 "every time Justin carried the ball. I didn't understand at first but I caught on quickly as Justin began laying good hits on this number 25 of the other team. This was the kid that had been brutalizing Justin in the first half. I know now what the coach had said at half time and it worked, Justin stopped taking the beating and began to dish it out now.

In the huddle the kids were congratulating each other for their hits. It wasn't points anymore, it had boiled down to who could hit harder and it was great. Our kids were getting more pumped over a hit than a score.

I recall watching the referees pushing the parents and the crowd back from the field as it was so intense they were encroaching the field. The half went on and even with the smallest success the crowd was going wild and chanting. The energy level at this field was higher and more volatile than I have ever experienced in my life it was as if the whole field was electric. I swear if the school behind us blew up and set ablaze from the blast no one at the field would have ever noticed.

The other team was the first to come out of the coma on the field near the end of the third quarter. They began to move the ball on our defense. It took a while and our decimated defense now held on as long as they could but the other team punched the ball through and scored to take the lead. Their bench and kids exploded with cheering and yelling as the struggle had broken.

Our Warriors were tired and beaten and I worried if our kids could hold on, the game was closing with little time left now.

The other team kicked the ball back to us and I went out on the field with the kids in the huddle. I looked at the kids and said.

"We have to suck it up now. I know this is tough kids but this is what makes champions of just normal players, we have to move the ball and score and I know that's not easy but we have to."

I put my hand in the middle of the huddle and told the kids, take the energy from me feel it and take it, I have lots to give. They put their hands in I told Kyle and Danny to start growling and screaming get angry kids and reach down deep.

I looked at Jess in the huddle and I could see in his eyes that he was there for me and this reassured me. I said.

"Justin take charge, all of you take charge of this game it's yours, you just have to go and take it."

I stood back as the kids lined up and ran the play. The kids were all screaming, growling now as they lined up and we began to get the looks from everyone and the kids began moving the ball and moving it well.

It was fantastic, we started the drive on our side of the field and with time running out and pumping and pushing we moved down to the other teams end of the field. The other team tried hard and fought back admirably but it was warrior time now and this drive was a classic. I recall on this drive that the other team was getting so frustrated with not being able to get at Justin to stop him because of the great blocking up front. The other team started getting this kid to leap frog over Jeff our center who snapped the ball to Justin. It was hilarious I watched this happen on a few plays and thought they must be desperate now as we were moving in to score.

About the third or fourth time this happened Jeff came back to the huddle all excited. Jeff looked at me and said.

"Hey coach do you see that kid, he's trying to jump over me." I smiled and said.

"Yes Jeff, I see it but I don't believe it I told Jeff".

"You are doing a fantastic job of stopping him son." I shook Jeff's hand, Jeff continued.

"All I'm doing coach is standing up and flipping him over me." I said.

"I know son and it's beautiful."

Jeff played center for us for four games and I never heard a peep out of him. He was a very shy boy but this day in this huddle the true Jeff came out and it was special to see, Jeff was so vibrant and alive now.

On top of the problem with the kid trying to leap frog over Jeff. The other team was sending in the infamous number 25 at Katherine's spot and he was getting through. It was like damage control on this drive. I looked at Kath and explained what was happening.

"This time Kath don't push on the block just stand still sweetheart and turn in the kid's direction and plant #25 into the ground." I looked at Justin and said.

"Call the play."

I stood back, Jeff flipped the kid and Kath flattened #25 as Justin tore up the field untouched.

We were now on the other teams 20 yard line and ready to score the refs were calling 3 minutes left, we were in the huddle and I remember the coach on our sidelines called a time out. I thought great we could regroup for the final minutes. We all huddled around and I put my hand in the middle and said.

"Come on kids take the energy, we have them on the run." The kids all put their little hands in and we all started to chant loudly.

"END ZONE, END ZONE."

I remember the head coach came out on the field to talk to us and all I remember was looking up at the coach as he looked into our huddle. As I knelt down with the kid's hands in and chanting the coach looked at me and shook his head and turned and went back to the sideline. He was later to tell me he wanted to talk with us but it looked like we had a séance going and he figured he better not bother us. I chuckled at him when he told me this after the game. Anyway in the huddle, I looked over at my little Jess and he tried hard to hide his pain but I saw that he was in pain and asked him.

"Jess, are you hurt?" Jess said.

"No" as he held back the tears and this killed me inside. I replied.

"Son, if you're hurt go off and send someone in for you, don't worry we can handle this team now." Jess refused to go off and I had such a hard time dealing with this. I snapped at Jess.

"If you're hurt, get off the field now before you get really hurt." It killed me to say this but I was worried about Jess.

Jess turned so stubbornly and walked to the sidelines. I do not think he realized but this motivated the hell out of all of us in the huddle as the rest of the kids witnessed their quiet leader. They knew Jess was refusing to leave the team and the field. Even when he was injured with all our other kids going off with injuries during this battle. Jess made us all look at each other and realize that we had to fight and fight we did. We came out of the huddle, ran our special play on this team, and blew them away with it.

We had 2nd down and six to go, we sent Danny out on a pass play we had practiced on our own. I stood back and Justin ran the play Danny made the most spectacular catch I have ever seen. He had about 6 of the other kids around him, meaning we didn't fool them at all. It was magnificent Justin threw the ball. Danny went up for the ball and in the mess of Viking defenders and he leaped up and pulled the ball out of the air and caught it amongst these 6 kids. It was truly a phenomenal play after the catch, Danny was so excited he fought his way out of the pile of kids with the ball in hand and ran back to us in the huddle just crazy with excitement. Danny jumped up on me hugged me and as he did he split my lip with his helmet.

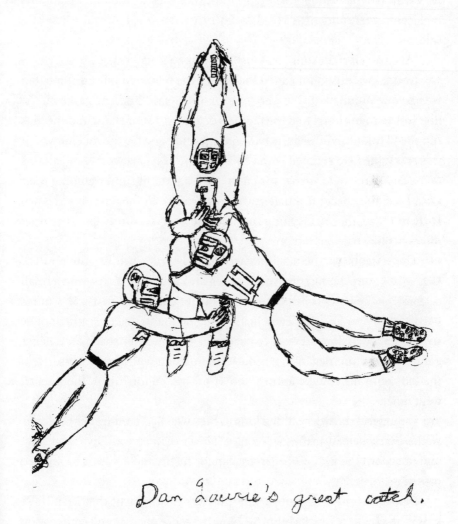

Dan Laurie's great catch.

The blood started to come out of my lip as I tried to talk to the kids in the huddle. Danny kept apologizing and I said.

"Don't worry son its now complete even the coach has an injury." As we all laughed we looked up as Jess came back in the huddle and his replacement left under the Head coaches instructions. I looked at Jess and said.

"Are you all right son?" Jess just looked and said, "I'm ready coach."

God, I love this kid. I called the play as the refs were yelling at me that we had one minute left. We were now on the 5-yard line, the game on the line and a minute left. I told the kids lets do it now, I stood back and the kids ran the play and slammed the ball into the end zone for the touchdown. It was crazy, the field erupted with cheering. The best part was we did all this at the end of the field where our parents were standing and watching their kids. I feel they became a true team now against all the adversity thrown at them today, these kids hung in there and tied the game up in the final moments like true champions.

The parents on the sidelines were all cheering wildly now and the kids and I were all hugging each other and celebrating. As we were all celebrating the parents began to call to our sidelines that Justin was hurt.

I looked over and there was Justin lying on the field at the same spot he scored the touch down. I went to head over but the other coach for defense got over there and began to comfort Justin along with the parents. I told the kids with me to take a knee and as we waited for Justin, the kids all went quiet.

I could feel the worry in the kids as they watched their leader go down, as the coach helped Justin to his feet. They began to walk by us without saying a word the kids all began to clap for Justin and stand as he walked passed us.

I looked at the kids and I think this was the moment that I felt these kids were now very much complete. Now the sense of pride and compassion for each other could not be matched by anything I had seen in this league.

After Justin was off the field I called the kids into the huddle. I looked at Danny and told him.

"You have to run the ball for us now, don't worry son we're all with you and we know you can do it, just follow the blocking. Are you ready? Danny, call the play."

I winked at Danny and patted him on the shoulder as I stood back. The refs were now calling three plays left in the game and the kids lined up and it was tense, the parents were all crowding this end of the field as Danny called out the play. The field went quiet and all you could hear was Danny's squeaking voice in comparison to Justin's barking the play and it happened, the kids smashed their way through and Danny walked into the end zone with relative ease.

Once again, the parents and the kids went crazy with their celebrating the game was now tied with a few plays left in the game and this meant overtime.

As I walked off the field with the kids, I noticed the other team and their coaches and it seemed like they had just had the wind knocked out of them. There was no more emotion or energy from their sidelines. This team thought they had my little Warriors beat. When I got to the sidelines I checked with Justin and he seemed all right. I think he was just winded on the play.

The ref blew the whistle and the game ended and we were headed to overtime, it could not get any better than this I thought to myself. It seemed like a fire drill on our sidelines as the coaches tried to get everyone's attention to prepare for the overtime period as the refs conferred on the sidelines and both teams were given a break period to get ready.

At this point, the refs were talking to the coaches of both teams on the field. As I watched I saw that the other two teams that were to play after our game were no longer in their practice squads. They were all huddled around this little field with the parents. It was incredible it was like the park was ready to burst with the amount of people enjoying this struggle. I thought to myself that it is time for the kids to shine.

The refs blew the whistle, our kids won the coin toss once again and we elected to receive the ball. The other team kicked and we ran out on the field like a bunch of wild animals. The kids and I were screaming and pumping it up as we got in the huddle. I told the kids.

"We have Justin back and this game is ours. We are going to win this game kids, now lets go out and do it and end this thing."

We all put our hands in the middle again and I said.

"Justin call the play" and as I stood back and watched and I yelled at Kyle and Danny.

"Come on kids, start growling get angry out there and start screaming." It was funny because as I said this Kyle and Danny began to scream like a madman and Dan began to swing his arms and start dancing on the spot. It was like he had ants in his pants it was so cute to watch.

The kids began to slam the ball down the field and as I had figured we marched the ball right down to the other teams end with no problem. Most importantly we ate up almost all the time, in the first overtime period. We stalled at the other teams 5 yard line.

The parents were all buzzing as they watched and our sidelines were going wild as they were yelling at me to watch the time. I looked at the ref and he told me there was only seconds left, so as we huddled and I told the kids the situation and said.

"I think we should kick the ball and get a single point before the first period ends."

The kids agreed, I did not think we would have had time to score if we did not make it on the first crack. I did not want to waste the kids' effort on the first drive. The kids lined up and Danny, being the kicker called the play. The ball never got to Danny as the snap was low the other team got in and covered the ball the first period ended, and we were still locked in a tie.

The ref blew the whistle and the kids and I headed to the sidelines. I reassured the kids on the way to the sidelines, I told them not to worry we were doing well and it was just a temporary set back. I got to the sidelines and one of the coaches was upset that we didn't go for the touchdown. I told the coaches it was my call and I thought it was the right call, it just didn't work. I then told the coaches not to worry we will get it back. We set up for the kick to the other team to start the second period. We kicked and our defense went out on the field to hold this team. We all cheered on the defense and it happened the defense turned the ball over to us fumble yahoo and we were all cheering. I ran out on the field with the kids we got in the huddle and I smiled and said.

"Let's smash face kids, the ball is ours, this game is ours, lets go take it Justin call the play."

I stood back and watched our little heroes again muscle the ball down field. We got down to the 10 yard line and we moved the ball into the other teams 3 yard line with second and goal to go. We huddled up and I asked the kids how they were doing. The kids all smiled and said good, I looked at the kids and said.

"Now lets slam this thing in the end zone and get the hell out of this zoo." The kids all smiled at me and we began to chant end zone, end zone. I told the kids to go do it, I stood back the kids lined up and the ref called to the teams three plays left. They ran the play and again the field blew up with cheering as Justin fell into the end zone for the touchdown and the lead, it was nuts. The refs were keeping the parents back off the field as the refs tried to keep control of the game. The kids and I were all dancing around and hugging each other. The ref called to me and demanded that I get the kids ready for the point after play as he tried to contain the crowd. It was field wide frenzy, I think for the first time the parents were really feeling the excitement of this journey.

I calmed the kids down, as did the ref with the crowd. We ran the play and scored the single point and we all ran to the sidelines yelling and screaming and celebrating. The sideline we could see was going crazy too awaiting our return. I was so excited, we were trying to hug each other and run at the same time and we were falling all over each other on the way back to the bench.

When we got back to the bench and the other coaches were scrambling to get the kids ready for the kick off and the two final plays in the game. We all focused in as we kicked and sent out our defense with us cheering them on. One play ran and our defense smothered it and nothing for the other team. The ref yelled final play, the kids all lined up and it went quiet. The other team called out its play and our defense got in on the other team and completely collapsed the whole teams offense. The ref blew the whistle and the field went crazy, it was over and the Warriors had just won the game of a lifetime and as well beat the top teams back to back wow wow and wow!

All I remember was one of the fathers of the kids ran right into me on the sidelines, grabbing me, hugging me and ranting "Warriors, Warriors," this man was big and it felt like a buffalo running into me as we were hugging. I could see the parents from the other side of the field were now running across the field towards us like a stampede of wild animals. They were running with arms out and screaming. I looked for the kids and thought, watch out kids here they come.

The father hugging me let go and congratulated me, screaming in my face.

"We did it, we did it." I said.

"Yes, we did I replied." I turned to find the kids and whack this other father ran right into me hugging and screaming in my ears.

"We did it, we did it."

I began to hug him and thought, what the hell it was time to celebrate now that the game was finally over. I looked at the man and thanked him for talking to the refs at half time. As the father ran off to find his son in the madness I turned and saw everyone congratulating each other. I headed into the pile of people trying to find Jess and as I did, I ran into Kim, grabbed her, gave her a big kiss, hug, and screamed at her.

"We did it, ma." Kim smiled and hugged me and said.

"Yes Sean, you did."

I let go of her and began to grab the kids one by one and hug them and congratulate them. Their little faces were full of excitement and pride, I loved it and these kids now were in a class of their own.

We all began to head over to the other side of the field, as the other teams were ready to start their game. As I walked across the field, I could see the frustration on the faces of the other coaches and the dejection in their kids. As our kids finally got away from the parents long enough to shake hands with this formidable team, we had beat. It was a somber acknowledgment from this team. I feel we had just broken the back of this fine football squad and it was great.

I turned to walk off the field and as I did, this little kid from the other team came up to me. His team left the field with out him and the kid looked at me and said.

"Hey coach, can I talk to you." I stopped and smiled and said.

"Sure son, come over here." As he walked to me, he smiled and he was so sweet he said.

"You know Katherine on your team." I said.

"Yes, I know Katherine." He then said.

"She's a good player, right coach." I laughed and said.

"Yes son, she's one hell of a good player and so are you son. It was a fantastic game and your team did very good." The kid smiled at me, turned and ran back towards his team.

I watched as the little one ran back and I thought how sweet that was of him then it hit me this was the kid Katherine had told me about at her school. I chuckled to myself and felt badly for this little kid, I hope Katherine did not upset this little guy too much. I watched as he rejoined his team and he turned back at me to wave. He was the type of kid we would have wanted on the squad. I turned and headed to the sidelines where the Head coach had Justin propped up on his knee as the parents and kids gathered for the speech afterwards. The cokes were flying and the energy was still electrifying. I stood and watched as the coach congratulated the kids and all the parents were glowing over their kids. As he spoke, I thought this is good I looked at Jess and as he looked at me I smiled and winked at him and he did the same. It is tough to explain the feeling of warmth that was coming over me at this time as I watched the kids and their parents so happy and so proud of their little Warriors.

These Warriors after this game I think must now be the favorites in the playoffs. Who would have figured this, it was a journey I knew would be destined for a championship. No longer will anyone talk about pushing these kids around on the field the talk would be on how to stop this little steam engine we had created. I turned back to this field and smiled and said to myself, you were not so intimidating after all cheers.

We all began to break up and head out as the other game was beginning. This was a morning and a game that I will never forget. Dave and I gathered the kids and headed to the car.

The kids were still yelling and chanting as we drove out of the park. I looked at Dave in the car and said.

"That was unbelievable buddy." Dave agreed and I then said.

"Dave, straight to the beer store and then get these kids home." Dave agreed. We got home and the kids ran inside with the video of the game. We put the tape on sat down and watched as Kim came in. She was still excited, she congratulated Dave and I on the victory and I could see Kim was now really getting into the kids and the journey. I was happy for her and the sons.

We watched the tape and began to unwind a bit as I don't know about everyone else but I was emotionally drained and exhausted. All I wanted to do was have a beer and relax.

I think this was when I first had the idea to possibly write the story about these kids and how they learnt about football and life so quickly and handled it. It truly was amazing to witness but I realized I had to wait to see how it turned out and if these kids could go all the way and complete this journey we began together. Were they true champions.

I believed so!

The Final Playoff Game of the Round Robin.

Practice rolled around again on Monday. When we got to the field the atmosphere of the kids, parents and coaches was one of great excitement still over Saturday's victory. It was good and well deserved for the kids. I gave the tape to the coaches and made my comments and there were no real recommendations as I told the coaches the team was now complete. As well, I felt invincible now.

The coaches were reluctant to agree because we still had two games to go. Yet, I believed in my heart that there was not a team out there, with the heart and character strong enough to even come close to these kids. We talked awhile and then the coaches called the kids in for warm-ups.

As the kids warmed up, the Head coach began to tell me the background of the team we just played and the reason for all the tension and animosity we were subjected to. The coach began to explain that the people in charge of that team used to be part of the Warrior organization. This woman had a falling out with the Warrior association, he did not go into the falling out and I'm glad he did not.

He continued to say that they blamed him and his teams for this mishap and there has been a type of off field feud between these teams and coaches ever since. I explained to coach that it was time for all involved to let go of the petty differences and remember that it's about the kids, not us. The coach agreed.

As we began practice I stopped and thought, great I was not crazy last Saturday the atmosphere and tension we felt was real and not in my head. The only thing that bothered me was that I should have been told about it before the battle not after it but I guess the coaches had their reasons. Practice went on well this week and everything was pretty upbeat.

The coaches, Dave and I began to discuss the playoffs the remaining games for all four teams involved. We all had one game left to play and our kids were guaranteed a birth in the final and all we needed to know was who was going to come dance with us.

The first team we beat the Bengals, I felt would be the team to make it to the final. The Bengals were at home this Saturday to the tough Viking team that we just beat and the winner of this game would meet us the following week in the final game. We talked and the coaches were of the opinion that the Viking team would beat up on the Bengals this Saturday and the Vikings would get the grudge match against us in the final.

I disagreed and told the coaches that our kids killed any spirit that the Vikings had in them and the Bengals would prevail. Of this, I was sure. I explained how emotionally upset the Vikings had been, and the bottom line in this game between these two teams. Was that both teams wanted another crack at us in the final and only one of the teams would get the chance. I told the coach it was too bad that we were playing this Saturday as I wished I could go to the Bengal field and watch this game and the coaches all agreed.

All we could do was wait and see what the weekend coming brought. As for our kids, we were to play the fourth and final team in this round robin affair and the team we faced were eliminated last week with two straight losses to the Vikings and then the Bengals. From what the coaches had heard, their losses were very lopsided. The coach began to tell me how we didn't have to worry about this team Saturday and that our kids would win easily and the game really meant nothing as we were in the final now. I heard this talk before and I did not like the results that this attitude brought us. I told the coach not to tell the kids this and that we were going into this game with the intent of taking this team seriously. No matter how bad they might be.

The coach laughed and said if our kids don't score in the game Saturday the game would wind up 0-0. I just looked and decided that I would just ignore this attitude this time and make sure that our kids would not be let down this time. I had many thoughts going through my head at this time and most of the thoughts were bad so I kept my tongue and we continued to discuss the playoffs.

Practice went on this week. We decided this week to take it a bit easy on the kids as they had worked hard to get to this position. Ingeniously, the Head coach decided that instead of practice on Thursday night, we would have a game of football, the coaches and the parents against the kids. The kids were wild about the idea.

I was excited about it too, but the only mistake of the coach was the timing. He chose the night that it was raining, muddy and cold. I thought to myself, well we expect the kids to play in it, so why not us.

We set up the teams after the coach got the kids all excited about hitting and tackling their coaches and parents. We lined up and I will say here that there were only a few of the parents who braved the task at hand and we were all grateful to those few.

We started by kicking the ball off to the kids and allowed them the first offensive possession as the ball sailed down to the kids. I will never forget this one parent he was the father that attacked the refs in our last game about the foul play. Anyway, this man tore down the field with reckless abandonment as the rest of us ran slowly dodging the puddles and the mud. This father tore right into the kids, hit the mud fell on his back, and slid for about 10 feet in the mud. As he slid he managed to get the ball carrier, tackled him and stopped the kids dead in their tracks on the return.

It was nuts I looked at the parent as he got up with mud all over him and dripping wet. I said.

"Great tackle." and he smiled.

The kids lined up their formation and Justin laughed at us as we lined up defensively. The kids ran the play and ran it well.

Well we tried to stop them even with Mean Joe Green playing for us. I jest, but you would have sworn that the father I refer to, was possessed as he went after the kids. It was fun to watch the kids score against us.

They kicked to us and we marched down field on the pass instead of the run and tied the game up and taunted the kids big time as we pranced around. I remember Dave and I kept laughing at the kids, saying you guys call this a defense.

The kids would get so pumped and angry and we would continue to tease, as the kids marched against us once again. The kids scored to take the lead and they teased and taunted us. We got the ball again and tied up the game and allowed the kids the final chance on offense to win the game and win the heathens did. I looked at the kids as we ended the game with their victory over us and complimented the kids on beating us with our own play. God did we the coaches and the parents take some ribbing over this as the kids took full advantage of the situation. They did deserve it these kids had worked hard for us more importantly for themselves.

After the game we all stood around just dripping wet and full of mud. We looked like a bunch of pigs wallowing around in the mud. The coach called practice and sent the kids home all full of mud and we chuckled, as we looked at the parents when they saw their kids all a mess. I remembered the father I talked about going crazy in the mud with the kids. I watched him as he left with his son and they climbed into this beautiful expensive car. Oh what a mess but it did not seem to bother the man. I really admired him, as he knew how to be a kid.

After the kids left the tiny park, we talked a bit about the game coming up and I applauded the coach for the idea of the mud bowl, although we got beat and soaked it was good. I believe at this point in the journey it was well needed, a bit of R and R for all. Dave and I gathered up the kids and limped home with them still teasing us. I never realized how hard these kids hit, we're fairly big men by most standards and these kids were dropping us like flies.

We returned to the little park on Friday night for the final practice before the game. The coaches and I talked as the kids played around and we all felt the same atmosphere from the night before should be continued tonight so practice was light on the kids. We ran through the basics once to keep the kids focused. We practiced the kicking game quite a bit as we were trying to perfect it and tomorrow's game would be a good time to work it. As the kids ran practice, the Head coach and I talked on the sidelines and we were on the same wavelength for tomorrow's game.

We were to take the game seriously until we had established a good lead in the game then we would let the kids have some fun. I thought this was a great strategy and we were both in full agreement on this. The coach called the practice, again we pumped the kids up and I demanded that the kids start heading to the zone now and bring it to me tomorrow and then we dismissed the kids for the evening.

Bzzzzzzzzzzzzzzzzzzzzzz. Saturday morning came and so did dad-slash coach-slash lunatic. I ran up the stairs and began the ritual of screaming and singing the fight song as the boys began to wake up and start to move around. I fed the boys and we got dressed and pumped at the same time in the usual fashion. I looked out the window and again the morning was beautiful. It was bright, dry and cool but not cold. I thought the Gods must be looking down on these kids, we had such lucky string of weather.

I took a moment here to reflect as I watched the boys prepare. I do that a lot reflect you know, but I felt the need as I watched Kurt and Jess prepare that we only had one more week of this journey and this season.

Soon it will all be over and though it was tough mentally, it was very rewarding and exciting to be a part of it. I knew in a week or two I would be missing these mornings of madness. I began to scream at the boys.

"Let's pump it up kids." I might as well make the most of it now, the boys were responding well to the craziness of their coach and it was a hell of a way to start your morning.

We got ready and headed out to the van to await Dave and his son as we were pooling it again. We ran over grabbed big bad Kyle at his house around the corner and got back to wait for Dave. We waited and we waited but no Dave. We pulled down the street and waited at the corner. I could not contain the kids in the van anymore, so we headed out to the east of the city and another adventure for the kids.

I began to enjoy these away games because I would make it a game in the van. I would tell the kids we were invading the other teams country and we were going to take over and leave our mark, the mark of the warrior. The kids loved this stuff, it really motivated them and it was fun. We used to scream in the van that we would not take any prisoners today. We will have it our way and only our way.

As the kids were chanting in the van, I again reflected to myself how much I was going to miss all this.

We got to the field, we were late and I noticed Dave's car in the parking lot. All was well and we were ready to play as we attacked the field with the kids. I could see Dave had the kids in full practice and I jumped right in with him ranting and raving with the kids. The other coach took over when we were finished and practiced the defense.

I walked over to the Head coach and took a moment to admire the field we were at today. It was a beautiful field, the sun was bright, and I saw all the parents lining up as they awaited for their kids to rule the field. I looked over at the other team practicing and their kids looked big, strong and prepared. It is going to be a good day for the kids, unlike last week I had a great sense of warmth and feeling from this field here. It almost welcomed me as I strolled over the grass this was the way it should be I said to myself.

I remembered I had forgotten the water bottles in the van so I headed off on my own to the van. As I passed the parents, one of them said.

"Good morning coach."

I turned and kind of whispered good morning back to the three parents standing there. I continued walking and the parent yelled at me.

"Hey, GOOD MORNING COACH."

I smiled at the parents and screamed back.

"GOOD MORNING, GREAT DAY FOR FOOT BALL EH."

I turned and began to run to the van and all the while thinking everyone is pumped now, even the parents are into this madness. I got the bottles and headed back to the kids. The game was about to begin now with the refs and the kids all ready. When the ref blew the whistle I recall the Head coach looked at me and said.

"Hey Sean, lets have some fun today, okay." I smiled and said. "We are, it's time to play."

We won the toss again, received the ball and began the offense. We went into the huddle, I looked at the kids and said

"Well kids, I think you know what to do now, Justin call the play."

I stood back and the kids began to move the ball down field, it took a little while and the kids scored. The game was on and the Warriors out in front.

We all celebrated the score. The other team prepared for our kick and set up their offense and we cheered on the defense.

The other team tried to run and the defense quickly took over the field. The coach called out for our offense. We got in the huddle and I began to take a complete hands off attitude with the kids. It was time to have a bit of fun. I told the kids in the huddle.

"You kids know what you're doing go ahead and do it."

I stood back, Justin broke the huddle and got the kids to line and then he began to bark out the play. It did not take long, the kids smashed through for their second score of the game, and it was still early in the game. We celebrated. We kicked the ball back to the other team and the defense took to the field again. The other team began to move the ball again but it was amazing this drive of the other team as we watched from the sidelines.

It seemed as though the other team would pick up a first down and yards and then on the very next play, they would get a loss of yards or a penalty. It was comical the kids on both sides were not sure what was going on. It seemed to me forever this drive but it never moved anywhere, the drive consisted of about 6 or 7 plays. After the other team finally lost the ball to our defense, I headed out to the field and I told the coach.

"All those plays and the ball is still in the same place."

I laughed. It was like the last 10 or 15 minutes never happened. I began to explain this to the kids and the kids all gave me that look, as if to say hey coach, who cares get your head in the game. I laughed at the kids and told Justin to call the play and I stood back ever so proud of the kids and watched as the kids executed another touchdown drive and took a commanding lead. As I watched, I thought to myself what have we created here? I tried to joke with the kids but it was all business with them. I thought the next drive, which would be undoubtedly in the second half as the half was closing the kids were going to have some fun.

We had the lead we wanted and this team was obviously not going to threaten us and if they did, we would deal with it. The Head coach was right this team was weak, and it was time for fun. We kicked the ball back to this team they ran the half out and the Warriors were well in control. Dave grabbed the kids and headed to the end zone for the speech and I headed to the coaches on the sideline.

We began to talk about the game and I told the coach, "You were right about this game and this team."

The coaches and I decided that the second half was for the kids and by no means would we try to rub the other teams noses in this defeat today. We stressed that they have fun and no humiliation to this other team what so ever. I began to tell the coach that the kids and coaches on the other team were a pleasure to play against even with our kids just blowing them away. The kids and coaches on the other side are still having fun and not getting nasty or angry with our kids and this I really respected.

When Dave brought the kids back for the second half, the coaches began to tell the kids that it was fun time and that no one will tolerate any teasing or taunting of the other team here today. In all honesty, I felt we had instilled this in our kids, mutual respect for the opposition as well as themselves. I think we just wanted to remind the kids of this. The second half began and it was fun and well deserved by both our kids and the other kids. The other team had just came through a horrible playoff round being defeated badly in their games. Our defense took to the field without the coach, as the coach told me the kids were going to run the half on their own.

The defense without the coach shut down this team right away and I ran out on the field with the kids to start the offense. I got in the huddle with the kids and knelt down in the middle of the kids. I looked up and smiled and said.

"Now have fun kids, who wants to run the ball?"

I was almost mobbed in the huddle as the kids all began to shout me, coach, me, I want to run the ball.

I tried to calm the kids down and eventually got some order in the huddle. I looked at Katherine our rock all year, I said.

"Kath, you first darling."

I quickly explained to her what to do and told Justin to hand the ball off to Katherine and I told the rest of the kids its time to block for Kath now. Justin called the play. I stood back and watched as the kids lead Katherine down the field, it was great. In the huddle I looked at Melanie and told the kids.

"Ladies first, Mel, it's your turn sweetheart. Don't worry Justin will give you the ball and you just follow these big boys." I pointed to Kyle and Danny. I said.

"They will take care of you out there."

I stood back and think I might have witnessed one of the most spectacular runs ever. Melanie was tall and lean, had long legs, just like a deer or fawn. She so gracefully zigged and zagged through the defense and made a fantastic run. Everybody was cheering when Mel came back to the huddle everybody was congratulating her on the run and she was so proud of herself. At this point now the coaches on the sidelines were getting into the fun as well as the parents on the sidelines.

The coaches were sending in all the kids one at a time and allowing all the kids on the team to be part of the offense today. We got down near the other teams end zone and in the huddle I looked at Bosco. One of our lead blockers that had went head to head with me off and on during this journey. I had promised Bosco the chance to score a touchdown I looked at Bosco and said.

"Now son you can have your touchdown. All three downs Bosco gets the ball until he punches it through." I stood back and saw that Bosco was happy and excited as I think he thought I had forgotten about his touchdown.

I watched as it took all three plays but on the third one he got in for the score and the celebrating began again. I watched Bosco, he was so excited and I was happy for him. We headed back to the sidelines and our defense now swarming on the field and took the ball away again. It was like a fever the kids were all having fun and getting into it.

I took to the field again and began to rotate the kids as ball carriers. It was very exciting for these kids to handle the ball in a real game as Justin normally carried the ball about 70 per cent of the time. The coaches had decided to give Justin a long overdue rest on the sidelines as the kids played Quarterback as well as running back. It was an excellent time for all.

I think the coaches on the other team as well as the kids could see what we were doing as the parents were all cheering on their kids and the atmosphere on the sidelines was one of ease and enjoyment. The team we were playing knew our record, as well, they knew their record and I am sure understood what was going on and knew we were not trying to run up the score on them. Believe me it was the furthest thought from our minds.

We got down to the other teams end zone again and I told Kyle, the lead blocker on the team it was his turn to score the touchdown. Kyle was a hard worker for this team and really deserved a chance to get some glory. I stood back and Kyle busted through the defense for his score. All in all most of the kids got to carry the ball one way or another.

The kids I had promised it to got their time and glory. I tried to get Jess to run the ball but for some reason he would not run it and this really hurt me. Jess is as I said very shy and I think his shyness got to him and that was all right with me. When Jess had to play, he was always there for the team and me and always gave 150 percent.

The game finally ended and the Warriors had won 39-0. It was the second shut out of this journey and it was too bad the game had to end as the kids were having so much fun. Even with the drubbing going on the kids on the other team seemed to get into the positive energy that was coming through on the field. It almost seemed that the kids from the other team were happy for us. It was quite the sight to see after coming through the first two playoff games. This team was a sheer delight to play and my compliments had to be given to those kids and their coaches. I truly respected them. After all the kids shook hands and the parents gathered for the speech, I wandered over to the other teams bench where the coaches were congratulating their kids on their play today.

I walked up and asked the coach if I could talk to them. The coach stood up and said sure.

I felt so good with this team and the coaches. I looked at the kids all huddled around with smiles on their faces and began to thank the kids for the game they had just played. I told them,

"The game was so clean and such a pleasure for me to play. Your season is now over but I look forward to meeting and possibly playing you again." I then concluded.

"From what I saw today, I'm sure we will meet you again in the playoffs." I thanked them, turned to the coach shook hands with the coach, and asked him if he understood that running the score was not our intention and I apologized for the score. The coach smiled and said.

"Hey, you got a great little team." The coach then thanked me for talking to the kids and wished us luck in the final game. I headed back to our sideline. You know as I write this book and replay this all in my head I constantly think about that team and their kids. They showed me the ultimate in sportsmanship in this league. I thought if you had to mold a team it be in their image.

As I headed back to our kids I watched as they all gathered and celebrated. These kids are undefeated in the playoff round 3-0. As I watched the kids dance and chant I thought to myself, this is by far one of the most pleasurable experiences in my life and an experience I shall never forget.

The cokes were handed out and the coach made a speech to the kids and I looked for Jess and when Jess and I made eye contact, I gave Jess the wink and the thumbs up and he returned it. I began to think as the coach spoke to the kids and parents, 6 games down and one big game to go. All that had to be done now was to win next week and this promise and journey will be complete. We all headed home and watched the tape of the game.

The kids were excited about this one as they completely dominated the game from start to finish and they all got in on the act on offense and really enjoyed the game. I looked at Jess, Kyle and Kurt as they sat there watching the tape and thought how fortunate these kids and how talented. I think more talented then they knew and watching now as winners was a true pleasure to me. I told the kids to look at me and I said.

"Today was fun? Right kids." They replied.

"Yes." I then said.

"Enjoy it boys but realize the job is not finished yet, we have one more game left to win and win we will, right boys?" The boys screamed.

"Yes coach."

I laughed and told the boys to enjoy and we would get back at it next week. I then told them that the coaches were going to call me when they found out who won the game between the Bengals and the Vikings. We all wanted to know who we would be facing in the championship game. The boys told me to call the coaches and I laughed said.

"It doesn't really matter who we face, right boys?"

Then the telephone rang and I got up and answered it. It was one of the parents of our kids and she had found out through the grapevine that the Bengals had defeated the Vikings this morning in their game. I thanked the mother for calling. I looked at the boys, and screamed.

"It's the Bengals boys." The boys began to cheer and I think the cheering was that they did not want to go through another tough game with the Viking team. I looked at the boys and said.

"It's Bengal time again." The boys began telling me how we were going to beat them again. Then Jess reminded me of the kid on the Bengal team that told Jess after we defeated them how his team would beat us in the cup final. I smiled at Jess and said.

"Hey give the kid credit, he knew his team would make it to the cup." I then said.

"But you know the sad thing is that we will have to burst the kids bubble once again. As well Jess, after we beat them that will be the time to just smile at that kid if you see him, right." Jess smiled and agreed.

I pulled out the videotape of the Bengal game, began to watch the tap and decided I might as well study the team and the formations and get a jump on next weeks practice. Until next week, folks.

Chapter 7

The Final Step

onday night's practice rolled around. We were all still excited about the winning, but I got this feeling from Jess a sense of determination or commitment. I think even the kids realized the magnitude of this week and the final game. I was kind of amazed at how the kids were behaving. We got to the tiny practice field that we all called home for the last 3 months. It was getting to be dusk now as we arrived at the field and the air was becoming cold and still. We got out and the boys ran off with their friends. I began to talk to the coaches who were, as I was dressed now in the layers of clothing needed for the season at hand. I handed the tape to the coaches of the last game and said I have no recommendations or comments. I said I felt that the kids were now complete and were playing at the top of their game.

The coaches chuckled and agreed. I told the coaches that I had also brought the tape of the first Bengal game and I wanted them to look at it this week for preparation. I told them that I had dissected the tape of the game all weekend and I then told the coaches from what I can see our kids will beat these kids again.

As the kids and the coaches got into practice, I stood back, watched and looked at the little park and I started to really feel the finality of this week and this journey. I saw that the hockey boards were now up in the park in anticipation of the winter and the hockey season. I thought to myself, God I wish this journey and season could go on forever. I looked over at the parents standing all huddled around on the sidelines beaming as proud as peacocks over their kids and their victories. It was a great scene and an even better reminder that all good things must come to an end one day and so shall this.

The coach called to me and woke me up and I began practicing with the kids. I kept making mental reminders to myself to try and enjoy this week for it was the last.

Next year, I would lose some of these kids to the upper levels of the Warrior program and may never have the opportunity to coach them again. One of these Warriors I knew was going up next year and I knew I would miss dearly was Jess.

Jess was too old now to be a tyke and I promised Kurt and Jacob I would be there for them, especially when Jacob first joins football. I figured I had better be there for him as I was for Jess.

Jess and I had talked about this earlier and we had agreed I would spend the time required for the other boys but when the chance came to move up and coach with Jess again I would jump at it and float back and forth with the other boys. You have to understand that Jess showed me the same passion for this game as I had and I wanted to stay with him. Kim made me aware that the other kids next year were expecting me to be there for them. Therefore, for the next while I told Jess I would attend all his games for sure. I reminded Jess you now know what it takes to be a champion just remember this little rag tag bunch your part of and what can be accomplished when you believe in yourself and have the courage to fight.

All right back to practice and the present. This week, we decided to drill the kids over the basics and create some real intensity. We worked on the kicking game quite a bit this week and the coach had a great idea. On Wednesday night, the coach decided to bring in the tape of the Bengal game and a T.V. We would set up in the tiny shack off to the side of the field and have a film night for the kids to try to familiarize the kids with this Bengal team.

Dave had suggested this from the very start, to take one night of practice a week and show the kids the tapes so they could see their strong and weak points. Dave kept saying it was easier to teach when you can make it visual for the kids. We told the kids to show up for practice and we were going to watch the tape they got all excited about the idea.

We pumped up the kids at every chance this week and the most impressive aspect of this week was it was almost like the kids knew the importance of this week. I really hope I'm not selling the kids short here but the kids took such a business like attitude to this weeks practice it was almost scary. The kids had taken over from the coaches and they would listen to us as we motivated and coached. Yet, I really had this sense that it did not matter whether or not the coaches were here this week, they knew what they had to do and they were doing it just like a well oiled machine. It was very impressive to watch.

Wednesday night rolled around and so did video night. We all showed up and held a quick warm-up with the kids and the coach set up the TV as the kids warmed up. We grabbed the tapes and headed into the tiny shack. We got them all in the basement and as expected along came the parents to watch the tapes. I laughed as we set up, I looked around and it was like sardines in a can, we were all huddled around with the kids sitting up front.

The tape started and we all settled in as the coach acted as narrator of the game. He was trying to highlight the strengths of the kids. All cheered on the kids for a second time as we watched. I stood in the back of the room and just watched and listened as he pointed out single kids and plays and congratulated them for the play. I thought, 3 more days, I could not wait. One of the kids made a comment to a play on the tape. The comment hinged on arrogance and I thought to myself that's good, they are confident and this little family I am now watching is about as close knit as it gets. To complete it all we could hear banging from upstairs in the shack, as some of the mothers were upstairs with the cheerleaders practicing for Saturday's game.

I think this was when I realized the love and caring of the kids coaches and parents, the little basement we were in was warm even though it was cold outside and the basement was damp and cold. The warmth I could feel was something from within I looked at the kids one at a time and remembered something special about each one from the last 7 weeks. Each had their own little character and the melting pot of characters was now at a good simmer and seasoned just right.

When the tape ended the coach asked the kids if there was any questions at all. We got questions all right, questions like what do we do with the cup when we get it. It was great, the kids were high. The coach dismissed the kids we talked a bit after everyone left. We further rehearsed the game, the final strategies and game plan. I will never forget when the coach looked at me and said.

"Hey Sean, I told the league to go ahead this week and put the Warriors name on the cup." I smiled and said.

"I told you it was a done deal." We laughed and I thought all right everyone is on board all we have to do is get to the dance on Saturday and end this journey.

We all showed up Friday night for the final season's practice. We drilled the kids and we pumped the kids but as I had mentioned, these kids seemed to be in their own little world all week.

The coach called to the kids and they huddled in with the parents. The coach began his final speech and he did a good job. The coach talked from his experience in the playoffs and the will to win and the passion to play. As I listened I said to myself, that's right coach cut to the chase just scream out the zone to them and they will completely understand and get the message. I then thought that's right, excuse me that's my job, sorry coach. We all had our chance to talk and when I got up there, I think the kids knew what was coming. After all the sensibility and wisdom and insight, it would all come down to one thing and when I got up there it came out. I walked up and looked at the kids sitting there and waiting for my madness I hesitated smiled and bellowed.

"WHO ARE WE?" The kids replied.

"WARRIORS." I screamed.

"WHAT DO WE DO?" The kids screamed back.

"SMASH FACE." I then furthered by yelling.

"WHERE ARE YOU KIDS HEADED TO RIGHT NOW?" The kids screamed out.

"THE ZONE, COACH." I then made it simple and yelled.

"BRING IT TO ME TOMORROW KIDS AND WE WILL KICK BUTT." After the parents and other coaches cleaned out their ears after the bellowing the coach dismissed the kids and it was sad to me as I watched the kids leave. I thought to myself lets stay focused Sean this thing isn't over yet.

As they left, the coaches, Dave and I gathered for our last time at this field to discuss any final thoughts on tomorrow. As we talked one of the coaches noticed how pumped I was getting and I told the coaches the only thing I had to say was "let's kick some butt tomorrow". They laughed and we called it a night. Dave and I gathered the kids, headed out and awaited the big game.

City Championship Game, the final step.

Buzzzzzzzzzzzzzzzzzzzz went the alarm and up and at em as I hit the buzzer, I shook myself awake. I looked in the mirror, gave that stupid smile, and screamed.

"Time For Some Football."

Up the stairs, I flew to find the slumbering troops as they lay strewn all over the living room floor. I stopped and looked out the window and realized that our string of luck with the weather had been broken, it was kind of overcast, and it was cold. I turned on the weather station, I sipped my morning coffee and decided to let the boys rest a bit longer before I began the madness.

The report said it was-27°C. with the wind bbrrrr I turned off the TV and looked again at the boys resting and I began to scream.

"Everybody up and get ready." The boys began to stir and like zombies began to rise as I was yelling in their faces. Jacob got up and headed for the solitude of his mother. I yelled at Jess.

"Lets get to the zone and get pumped and ready, for today is the day." As we headed to the field, I began to reflect a bit as the kids were driving each other crazy, I looked in the rear view mirror at these little tigers and thought I don't even think these kids realized what they have accomplished.

I screamed as we walked on the field together.

"IT'S A GREAT DAY TO WIN A CHAMPIONSHIP" and the boys began to chant As the kids walked, I looked up at the sky and I saw that the sun was slowly busting threw, and I thought that maybe our luck had not run out.

Once again we were the first to arrive and the field was so peaceful. I knew it was only a matter of time before the final time this year the field would awake to the two teams and the parents and the bustle of the game. As they walked the field, I smiled and screamed.

"WHO ARE WE." The boys screamed back.

"WARRIORS." I then screamed.

"Get it up kids, start finding the zone now."

As we walked, Dave showed up with his son and Dave was as ready as I was to pump up these kids and take home the championship. We began to get the kids together as they trickled in on the field. We began the warm-ups with the kids and we both knew we had to keep the kids moving around in order to keep them warm in this arctic like setting. I looked at Dave and said the sun is fighting to get out, if it breaks through it might warm up some. Most of the kids were here now and I felt sorry for them it was so cold but they seemed to handle the cold really well so far.

I think the kids were once again in the zone and ready to play as I watched their little faces in their helmets with their war paint on and their eyes coming into focus.

Dave had the kids doing their warm ups as I walked through their ranks looking into the eyes of these Warriors and winking as I bellowed.

"GOOD MORNING."

The kids wouldn't even smile at me and I thought to myself, we have created little monsters here. Well Dave continued the warm ups as I continued to motivate the kids. I noticed the other team the Bengals had arrived now and were doing their warm ups at the other end of the field and the stands were beginning to fill with the parents and spectators. It was a good feeling to see so many people come out to brave the cold and watch their kids do battle today.

When we finished the warm ups we tried to keep the kids moving and then the other coaches arrived and took over from Dave and I. We headed over to the sidelines to greet some of our friends who had come out to watch. We stopped and said hello as the other coaches took the kids into the locker room for the final pre game speech of this Cinderella season.

As the kids all marched passed us to the rooms I looked up at the crowd and wondered how many of our kids' parents could believe that we were here today. I chuckled to myself and Dave asked me.

"What was so amusing?" and I replied.

"Nothing."

As we talked, I kept looking to the clubhouse and wondering what the other coaches were saying to the kids. I noticed that the field was all set up now and the league officials and the refs were getting ready to start. The

Bengal team was in the other side of the clubhouse awaiting the start of today's match. I looked at Dave and said.

"We better get in there and see what's going on," Dave agreed and we headed over to the clubhouse. As we entered the room where our kids were, all I could remember thinking was who died, it was like a tomb. The coach was having a heart to heart with the kids. He was telling the kids the formula for success in the finals and sharing his experience with them.

I began to walk around the room and look into their eyes as I passed. I would wink and give that stupid smile and they would just looked at me with an intensity we had all become accustomed to now. The coach continued to talk as I moved quietly around the room I looked at the other coach, who was standing at the door and I gave him that stupid smile, then I looked at Dave and gave him the same smile. He began to shake his head and smile at me because he knew what was coming.

I turned quickly and looked at Danny. I couldn't take it any more, it was too quiet. I know the kids must have been wondering because this close to a game I was usually a raving lunatic. As I looked at Danny and he looked back and I screamed at the top of my lungs.

"WHO ARE WE?" the room exploded with the kids all screaming back.

"THE WARRIORS." I then screamed.

"AND WHAT ARE WE GOING TO DO TODAY?" The kids all replied.

"SMASH FACE COACH." I then furthered.

"WHERE ARE YOU KIDS NOW?" The kids screamed back.

"THE ZONE COACH." I then screamed.

"Get in the zone, get it pumped and lets go out there and kick some butt today." Now I was happy, the all familiar frenzy had started, the kids were all screaming and slapping each others pads. I didn't mean to interrupt the Head coach but it was almost game time and the other team was next door and I wanted them to know we were here and we were ready. As we were screaming, I thought the paint is on their faces, the song will be sung, the journey is about to be complete, our kids were headed to the zone, the craziness was going, and I was happy. The head coach called to the kids to the field now and we all ran out the door like a bunch of lunatics looking for trouble. We headed to the field and I remember the coaches giving me that look of bewilderment as I ran with the kids yelling and screaming with them.

We got to the field, I could see that the stands had filled now with spectators. It was great as I crossed the field with the kids, one of the coaches came up to me and began to tell me that I shouldn't get upset if things didn't go well today for the kids. I looked at the coach and said.

"Don't worry, we are here to win today, so don't worry." The coach persisted with me about not getting angry and I could not believe after all these kids had done how any one could not believe in them. I looked at the coach and said.

"Don't worry about it just, hold on for the ride." And I walked away.

We had a game to play, and it was time to get to the zone. As I walked away, I thought all I wanted now was to be on the field with the kids, begin this battle and prove to everyone how great these kids are. I thought the time for worry and talk was over now, it was time to smash face period. I knew above all else that the kids understood me and understood what had to be done here today. All I wanted was to be on the field with the kids so that we could climb into that little world together that we called the zone, and play ball.

I remember looking over at the Bengal team our opposition today as they came out on the field to meet us, the kids on the Bengal team looked to me like they wanted revenge today. I laughed to myself thinking you kids think you are going to come out here and rule ha!

As I roamed the sidelines awaiting my call, I looked at Jess and gave him the thumbs up and a wink and Jess returned the gesture. I then looked over at the cheerleaders that my wife Kim and her helpers were organizing for the teams cheering today. The girls were so cute. I then heard an announcer beginning to announce the teams and the day's events. I thought to myself this was big time football now we had everything as well as an announcer calling out the kids' names as he introduced the kids to the crowd.

As I watched, I began to tell the kids to run out on the field after they announced their names and scream "WARRIORS", and the kids began running out on the field with arms raised. It was just like college football in the south other than the blistering weather we had to contend with.

After all the kids were on the field, I heard them announce my name and I ran out on the field with my arms up screaming "WARRIORS" and the kids loved it.

We were all set now. The refs were on the field calling in the team captains for the coin toss, this was it, all the practice and work was over and the last 7 weeks all boiled down to this one game. The coach looked at me and asked.

"If we win the coin toss, do we want the ball first." And I replied.

"Of course coach, it's time to SMASH FACE", he shook his head and smiled. Justin, the team captain turned to us as he won the toss on the field and he knew that if we won, we wanted the ball first. It was now tradition, if we get the ball first and we score first.

The Bengals kicked the ball to us and we set up on about our 20 yard line, the coach called to me and I ran out on the field with the kids and we set up the huddle.

In the huddle I looked at the kids and I growled and said.

"Let's do it kids, we're here where we wanted to be and all we have to do is Smash Face one more time". I then told the kids.

"This Bengal team that we faced today wanted to beat us bad so we had to give all we had today, no sleeping on the job." I smiled and told Justin.

"Call the play son." And I stood back and watched as the kids lined up and tried to move the ball against this very stubborn Bengal defense.

We tried twice to move the ball but were unsuccessful in doing so and I told the kids in the huddle.

"We have to kick the ball and try to force this team back and let our defense shut them down."

We ran the punt play and Danny got off a great kick and moved back this very determined Bengal team, they recovered the ball around their 40 yard line and set up their offense. Our defense headed out on the field and we all slapped hands as we passed each other on the field. We were cheering on the defense from the sidelines as the Bengals lined up their offense and began their plays and they began to move the ball relatively easy against our defense. It was obvious that this team really wanted to beat us today as they came at our kids right from the start.

The Bengals moved the ball down to our 20 yard line and all of our sideline went quiet as they seemed to be doing to us what we normally did to other teams, control the ball. The Bengals Went on 3rd down and short to get the first score and we all held our breath as the quarterback dropped back to throw the ball. It was the exact play that we had remembered about this team and practiced the kids on all week.

We watched and at the last possible second, Katherine was obviously listening in practice this week because she got in just in time to break up the play. We sighed with relief and then began to chant Warriors and Katherine as the defense ran to the sidelines and the kids and I took to the field again for the offense. We made special efforts to congratulate Katherine as we passed on the field for her spectacular play.

We set up the huddle and we could hear the defense on the sidelines now cheering us on, I looked at the kids and said.

"Come on kids, we have to move the ball, we are pinned in our end and we have to get some field position back. We can't rely on the defense to save our necks we have to help them, so lets go out and smash face." Justin called the play and I stood back as the kids ran the play. Once again we tried but the field was so slippery from the snow and our offense depended very much on good footing, well we tried again and were unsuccessful in picking up a first down. In the huddle I looked at the kids and said.

"Come on kids if we can't move this team lets at least get a good kick off and back them up for the defense."

We broke the huddle and I stood back and watched as Danny and the kids got off a great kick and backed up the Bengal team to about their 30 yard line. We were slowly gaining back some field position but the kids were slow. It was either the footing, the cold or any number of things not excluding the excellent play of the Bengal defense.

As I walked back to the sidelines I shook hands with the defensive coach as we passed and all the kids cheered on the defense as they took to the field. The Bengal offense set up again and as did our defense and the Bengals began to move the ball against our kids again and I could feel everyone on our sideline were becoming very concerned. You know I never felt any sense of urgency or panic from the kids, it was amazing they were continuing on like normal, almost in a robotic fashion. But I know everyone else on the sidelines were worried.

The kids had a calming effect on me as I watched them on the sidelines and on the field. I thought to myself, although we are in tight the kids still believed. I watched the field as once again their offense gave everyone reason to be concerned as the Bengals marched the ball well against our defense.

I focused on our kids on the field and on the sidelines they were confident and seemed unfazed by the events going on. The Bengals marched to our 20 yard line and I remember cheering the defense and I was yelling at Katherine and Jess, trying to pump them up from the sidelines.

I also remember thinking, please kids hold them don't let them take the lead on us. It was now turning into a real struggle of wills on both their kids and ours. Well it happened again the Bengal team turned over the ball near our end zone and our defense came up big thank God.

I ran out on the field with our kids to set up the offense and the first quarter was coming to an end and as far as we could see there was no score but the Bengal team was dominating the game, something we were not accustomed to.

We got in the huddle and we changed ends of the field as the first quarter expired I looked at the kids I had become so close to and asked.

"Hey, what's the scoop, you're letting this team take it to you what's wrong with you, this is not the Warriors I have come to know. Come on kids let's start pushing these kids out of the way" and I began to yell in the huddle.

"LETS SMASH FACE". I looked at Kyle and Danny our lead blockers and told them.

"Start getting angry out here, let's start growling and screaming and start SMASHING FACE here." I told Justin

"Call the play," I stood back and watched, the kids ran the play and low and behold the kids began to back up this very stubborn Bengal defense.

In the huddle I told the kids.

"That's the way, I know these kids are tough but you got to get angry and take what you want because they are not going to give it to you. So pump it up kids and get angry and move them."

It was comical once again. They began screaming and growling before the play and the refs on the field and the other kids and coaches began giving us that look of disbelief.

As the kids started getting ready to smash face, they ran the play and picked up the first down. The parents were cheering and so was I. Our sidelines were cheering us on and in the huddle I told the kids.

"That's it, look in my eyes and feel the power kids, get out there and show them how to smash face." Justin called the play and I stood back and watched as we managed our second first down our kids were beginning to get their feet now.

We moved the ball pretty well but the Bengal defense were not ready to roll over and die and we were stopped about mid field as we set up for the kick. I told the kids in the huddle.

"Don't worry kids we moved the ball well, we have to be patient we have gained back good field position now. Let's try the fake kick and see if we keep this drive alive." The kids agreed. We called the play, I stood back and watched as they ran the play but the Bengal team read it well and shut it down and forced the defense on the field, and we left the field.

On the sideline I looked at the Head coach and told him.

"Don't worry, we were getting the offense going, just be patient with us." The coach smiled and said.

"All right Sean."

We began to cheer on the defense and it happened. The Bengal offense turned the ball over to us, our defense recovered as our sideline went wild with celebration. I ran out on the field with the kids, and we took time to congratulate the defense as we passed. The ball was about mid field, it was our ball, the first half was almost over and there was still no score.

I got in the huddle with the kids and I put my hand in the middle of the huddle and told the kids.

"Put your hands in and feel the power." I was getting really pumped now and I wanted the kids to meet me in the Zone I said.

"Get there, I'm in the Zone, come meet me, get angry and get pumped and let's move this ball." Justin called the play, I stood back and watched and the kids took my lead. They began to move the Bengal kids out of the way the kids were beginning to smash face now and I think the Bengal team and coaches knew it as they had seen this before about 3 weeks ago. We moved the ball down to around the Bengal's 20-yard line and now the kids were slowly taking control back from the other team.

It happened with about 2 minutes to go in the first half, I said to Justin.

"Call the play" and I stood back and watched one of the most spectacular runs and solo efforts I had ever seen. Justin called the snap, took the ball right as the play was designed to go right but right in mid play Justin reversed the play and went the other way. He caught everyone off guard and broke three tackles as he romped into the end zone for the first major of the game. After he scored he did his patented little dance in the end zone, the field blew up with cheering from mostly the stands where all the parents were watching. It was great, we had the lead 6-0, we tried the point after, again we missed and we left the field to our defense and little time left in the first half.

The Bengal offense came out and moved the ball well against our kids but fortunately for us the half ended just as the Bengals were threatening to score again. The ref blew the whistle and the first half was over with the warriors leading 6-0 and beginning to take the momentum away from the other team.

I was so proud of these kids they were so pumped that in the first half of this game Danny made a mistake that cost us field position. As Danny came off the field he broke down and began to cry, I walked up to Danny and said.

"Hey son, don't cry we all make mistakes and your not the first or the last to make one, but son you can't cry about it. You have to be strong and suck it up and realize that no matter what, your team depends on you, you have to get passed it and get back to your team." I finished by telling Danny that he knew he could play and we knew he could play and all he had to do was go out and play. Danny smiled, rejoined his teammates and this is what these kids were made up of, true fighters to the end. They were no longer looking like the misfits they were once labeled to be.

The coaches called the kids over as the Bengal team headed into their locker room for the half time break, the sun now had come out and was beginning to warm things up a bit.

I was amazed at how the kids were holding up to the cold weather, the coaches debated over bringing the kids in for half time to warm up or keep them outside and keep them used to the cold. Well the decision was to keep the kids outside for if they went inside they would only freeze again when they came out. Therefore, Dave took the kids into the end zone for his usual half time speech to rally the kids and the coaches and I conferred on the sidelines about the game. We talked and I told the coaches that we were going to try this new twist on offense that we had developed this week in practice just for this team.

The coach knew the twist and agreed it was simple. We decided to change the position of our lead blockers, Danny and Kyle, the other team knew wherever these two lead blockers went, so did the play. I believe this is why the offense was so slow in the first half. The coaches on the other team were sending their kids to where Danny and Kyle were going. The twist was we would send the lead blockers one way and on the snap of the ball then we would run the opposite way. We decided to give it a try in the second half.

Dave brought the kids back and they were all pumped and ready. Once again we had the new strategy and we were ready for the second half. The refs were on the field and so were our kids. We were ready but the Bengals were no where to be found. I approached the refs on the field and I remember hearing someone from our sidelines yelling out.

"I think they went home" Just as he said this, the Bengals came back out onto the field and looked pumped and ready to go.

I went back to the sidelines as we had to kick to them to start the second half. We lined up and kicked the ball to the Bengals and they set up offence with their offense deep in their own end. It was at this time our defense was taking to the field and one of the parents came up to me and said.

"Hey coach, come take a look at this kid over here", I turned and looked and saw a bundle of Warriors capes and blankets up on the sidelines, it looked like a little pile of laundry. The parent directed me to this little pile and all the time I was trying to follow our defense on the field and the game. When I got to the pile, I knelt down and pulled the clothes up and there was Kurt's little face, all white from the cold. I looked at Kurt and said.

"Are you okay?" I smiled at him Kurt just nodded his head. I picked up Kurt, began to cuddle him, and told him.

"Everything would be all right I told Kurt." I looked at the parent and asked if he would take Kurt over to the other side of the field and find his mother and she would take him inside. He agreed and I knew and trusted this parent. He lifted Kurt from my arms and began to walk away. As he walked away, I remember feeling this sense of helplessness because I felt I should be with my son. At the very same time the coaches were calling to me to take the field with the offense as our defense just turned the ball over again. I looked at the coaches then I looked at Kurt and it tore me up but I trusted the parent and I had to return to the kids.

I thought, my God its tough to be a coach when it was time to be a father. I knew Kim would soon have Kurt and take care of him. I ran by the coaches as the kids and I took the field as I headed out the coach looked at me and said.

"Okay Sean lets take it home now." I got in the huddle, and I was pumped. I looked at the kids with faces all painted and their eyes focused on me and I said.

"Let's smash face kids, lets take this ball and ram it down their throats and show these kids what the Warriors are all about." I yelled at the kids in the huddle.

"Are you with me?" and the kids replied.

"Yes coach." I then said.

"Let's go do it, Justin call the play." I stood back and watched as our kids began to take over. The kids were moving the ball and moving it well. We got down around the Bengals 30 yard line with some good aggressive blocking and some true heart. We got in the huddle and it was second down and about 5 yards to go and we were going in. In my mind, we were going in to score and really open this game up. We had the rhythm, we had the flow and I now felt these Bengals could not stop us anymore.

I told Justin to call the play in the huddle and I stood back and watched. As Justin barked out the play, Bosco jumped offside and the ref threw the flag, it was a penalty against us. I couldn't believe it, Bosco was one of the few experienced kids we had and this was unthinkable for him to do.

We got back in the huddle, I looked at Bosco and I said.

"Son get your head in the game, you're a veteran to the game you can't make mistakes like that and you know it. I expect that kind of stuff from the many young kids we have not you son." I then looked at Bosco and said.

"You owe your team big time son, we were going into score." The rest of the kids in the huddle went quiet, I did not mean to center him out but it was wrong what he did and we all knew it. I looked at Justin and said.

"Come on kids let's try and get the first down, pump it up." I stood back and the kids tried hard but couldn't do it and we turned the ball over to the Bengals at what I felt to be a crucial point of the game. As we headed back to the sidelines, I saw the parent who took Kurt and I asked if he found Kurt's mother and he said.

"Yes" and I felt a lot better. I looked over at the Head coach and said.

"Other then that penalty we would have moved in for the score." The coach agreed and told me not to worry about it, we began to cheer on the defense as once again they began to dominate.

The defense found their legs and were shutting down everything the other team was trying to do. Then it happened, the Bengal offense ran their pass play and as we watched the quarterback drop back for the pass again, he threw the ball up and this time it was Bosco who had listened during practice. Bosco ran under the ball caught it and ran about 30 yards into the end zone for the score. Wow it was now Warriors 12-0 the field went wild with cheering. I could not believe it, it was Bosco. I don't think you could have scripted it any better for the kid, we all ran out on the field and began to mob Bosco. I grabbed him, hugged him, and said.

"Beautiful play son, we are all even on the debt." We shook hands and smiled and the kid was on top of the world now.

We took to field and set up for the point after and I recall looking over at the Bengal bench and you could see the frustration and dejection in the kids and the coaches. I felt bad for them, we were good on the single point and we all celebrated as we took a 13-0 lead with the third quarter ending, we kicked the ball back to the Bengals.

The day got brighter in more ways than one. The sun came out on our kids once again and the Warriors defense completely shut down this rival team and the offense went on in true Warrior fashion to score twice more. The new twist on offense worked like a charm and we ran the ball at will through the rest of the second half.

Every time we went to run one way, the Bengals would set up for that way and with the twist we would run the other way catching them completely off guard. The Warriors went on to win the game 25-0 and pitched another shut out. These kids were invincible now, and I think all knew it. I was very appreciative of the professional manner the Bengals took the defeat. It was a long tough battle fought by both teams.

Our little Warriors rose to the top of the game and imagine about 7 weeks ago these kids were about to be written off for the season. I guess nobody took into account the hearts of these little kids, for it was their heart and their courage that got them here as city champions. Not only did these kids win one game, they won six of seven games and made a clean sweep of the playoffs.

When the game ended so did this Cinderella season and when the whistle blew to end the game, we all charged the field and the kids. I stood back and watched as the kids all mauled each other on the field. It was a beautiful moment to witness and as this was going on, I saw Kim bringing Kurt back over to our sidelines and I yelled to him to come and celebrate with his team mates. He ran right in, the journey was over and the promise fulfilled thank god.

I looked around for Jess in the mess of bodies of both kids and parents, when I saw him. I caught his eye and I gave him the final wink and thumbs up. Jess, while celebrating with his teammates returned the gesture with a smile and all was complete for me now.

The promise I had made was honoured and my son was happy and his team were champions now. As the kids shook hands with the other team I walked along, shook hands complimented the Bengals on their valiant effort today, and thanked their coaches for a well played game. After this we headed to the center of the field where the trophies were being handed out and we lined up.

It was a moment I will never forget as the league officials brought out the huge Trophy and handed it to our little Warriors and the cheering and celebrating began all over again. I stood back and watched the kids revel in their success and I held back the tears because this bunch of kids had proven to me and so many others that your dreams are within reach. All you have to do is want it and believe in yourself enough to go out and get it.

These kids dreamed about winning a game and to try and get up and fight like a Warrior. Like a Warrior they did arise and win, at one time it was just a dream and these kids turned their dream into a reality.

The kids, the parents and the coaches danced around the field, pictures were taken and finally we were lead off the field for the next two teams to come on.

As the kids and parents headed over to the tent for pizza and coke, Dave and I made a quick exit to the parking lot. We stood and talked for a bit and we had arranged to meet at home later to celebrate.

Dave headed out and I turned and looked at the field that had been so good to the kids and I, for it was this field that we began this journey together some 7 weeks ago. It was the same field where we ended this journey today much in the same fashion. I looked at the field, tipped my Warrior cap to it and thanked it for being so good. I turned and headed to the car and stopped to realize that I had one more person to thank and that was my deceased mother Rose. I had privately dedicated this game and these kids to her memory. I knew that some where my mother was watching my kids and I and she was gleaming from ear to ear. Watching her son and her grandsons display and exercise the true Graham in us all.

I then turned and walked away!

Conclusion

*I*n closing, this story and this magical chapter in my life and this journey with the kids inspired me to write this story. These kids inspired myself and themselves to believe that anything is possible if you have the confidence and the willingness to fight. Along with this a life lesson was learnt and savoured by all that were involved.

It was my honour and privilege to write this story and allowed to be part of these kids and their dreams. Hopefully in some small way, this book may reflect on the magical season of the 1996 Warriors in our hearts and in our mind. As for Jess, he now stands on the very same field coaching his little tykes on their journey some 20 years later. I watch Jess and his kids and I feel so proud of him. I hope with all my heart that he and his kids can have a magical year together.

Printed in the United States
By Bookmasters